Fiscal Policy and Environmental Welfare

NEW HORIZONS IN ENVIRONMENTAL ECONOMICS

General Editor: Wallace E. Oates, *Professor of Economics, University of Maryland*

This important series is designed to make a significant contribution to the development of the principles and practices of environmental economics. It includes both theoretical and empirical work. International in scope, it addresses issues of current and future concern in both East and West and in developed and developing countries.

The main purpose of the series is to create a forum for the publication of high quality work and to show how economic analysis can make a contribution to understanding and resolving the environmental problems confronting the world in the late twentieth century.

Recent titles in the series include:

Fiscal Policy and Environmental Welfare

Modelling Interjurisdictional Competition

Thorsten Bayındır-Upmann

Assistant Professor, Institute of Mathematical Economics, University of Bielefeld, Germany

NEW HORIZONS IN ENVIRONMENTAL ECONOMICS

Edward Elgar

Cheltenham, UK • Northampton, MA, USA

Published by
Edward Elgar Publishing Limited
8 Lansdown Place
Cheltenham
Glos GL50 2HU
UK

Edward Elgar Publishing, Inc.
6 Market Street
Northampton
Massachusetts 01060
USA

A catalogue record for this book
is available from the British Library

Library of Congress Cataloguing-in-Publication Data
Bayındır-Upmann, Thorsten, 1965–
    Fiscal policy and environmental welfare : modelling
  interjurisdictional competition / Thorsten Bayındır-Upmann.
    Rev. version of the author's thesis (doctoral—University of
  Bielefeld) presented under the title: Interjurisdictional
  competition and environmental policy.
    Includes bibliographical references.
    1. Public goods—Mathematical models. 2. Government competition–
  –Mathematical models. 3. Fiscal policy—Mathematical models.
  4. Environmental impact charges—Mathematical models.
  5. Intergovernmental tax relations—Mathematical models. I. Title.
  HB846.5.B39 1998
  336.2—dc21   97-44512
                                                              CIP

ISBN 1 85898 738 5

Printed and bound in Great Britain by
Biddles Ltd, Guildford and King's Lynn

Contents

Figures and Tables

FIGURES

TABLES

Preface

This book represents a revised version of my doctoral thesis which was originally submitted to the University of Bielefeld under the title *Interjurisdictional Competition and Environmental Policy* to apply for the degree of Doctor in Economics in April 1996. In the meantime, parts of this work have already been published in some journals. Namely, Chapter 2 encompasses results contained in an article forthcoming in *International Tax and Public Finance*, 5;* Chapter 3 is based on an article forthcoming in *European Journal of Political Economy*;† and Chapter 4 draws on an article published in *Finanzarchiv*, 52 (NF), 1995, 379–400.‡

I am indebted to Till Requate whose comments and criticism inspired and improved a substantial part of this work. Moreover, my thanks are due to my advisers Walter Trockel, Institute of Mathematical Economics, University of Bielefeld, and Gerhard Schwödiauer, University of Magdeburg, for supporting me and making this work possible. Furthermore, I have to thank Susanne Klimpel and Willy Spanjers for useful comments and for pointing out idiosyncrasies in the English language.

This work has also gained from presentations at the EAERE meeting in Umeå (Sweden), at the IIPF congress in Lisbon (Portugal), and at a workshop in Ede (The Netherlands) as well as from presentations at the Universities of Bielefeld and Konstanz.

My special thanks, however, are dedicated to my wife, Inci Bayındır, who provided me, at all times, every conceivable support.

*Published by Kluwer Academic Publishers, Norwell, MA. See Bayındır-Upmann (1998a).

†Reprinted from Thorsten Bayındır-Upmann (1998b), 'Interjurisdictional Competition in Emission Taxes under Imperfect Competition of Local Firms', *European Journal of Political Economy*, **14**, (forthcoming), with kind permission from Elsevier Science - NL, Sara Burgerhartstraat 25, 1055 KV Amsterdam, The Netherlands.

‡See Bayındır-Upmann (1995).

1. Introduction

Within the last decade politicians and economists have raised the question of whether competition among jurisdictions enhances efficiency or not. Unfortunately, the scientific debate up to now does not satisfactorily illuminate this challenging topic, and the implications of intensified competition in the public sector are not yet sufficiently elaborated. While one strand of the literature argues that interregional competition increases efficiency, the other part raises its voice in warning of destructive competition. The optimistic view rests upon the model of Tiebout (1956) and the related literature: each individual household , drifting across jurisdictions, resides in that region that offers, from its individual viewpoint, the best policy bundle. By 'voting with their feet', citizens urge local governments to provide public goods efficiently. On the contrary, the more pessimistic strand contends that local governments, fearing capital flight and the loss of jobs, tend to lower tax rates. If this turns out to be true, interjurisdictional competition ends up with too low tax rates and too little provision of public services. Similarly, governments seek to attract firms and to create new jobs by lowering environmental standards. Thus, interjurisdictional competition not only leads to underprovision of public goods but also to excessive environmental degradation ('ecological dumping').[1] Consequently, the latter view calls for intervention of a higher level government to regulate interjurisdictional competition.

Empirically, the establishment of major, shared taxes, as for example in Germany,[2] reflects the endeavour to mitigate disruptive interregional competition. Analogously, the attempt to harmonize the major EU tax rates before full competition (the 'single market') is set up originates from the same fear. On the contrary, the US member states face almost no restrictions on their taxing power. The resulting tax competition leads to relatively low state and local tax rates. However, in the US case, interjurisdictional competition is defused by immense intergovernmental grants.[3]

Free and unrestricted interregional competition has not been established anywhere, even though, in this polar case, the answer concerning

1

the efficiency of interjurisdictional competition is easily found from the theoretical viewpoint: under the ideal conditions of perfect competition, efficiency is guaranteed. However, if any of these conditions is not met, the efficiency implications of governmental competition may become ambiguous and vague. Moreover, if local governments do not have unlimited access to head taxes (and lump sum transfers), they have to rely on distortionary taxation which destroys Pareto efficiency, in general. If poll taxes are not available, the remaining fiscal instruments have to serve several purposes: correcting market imperfections (on the input and on the output side), regulating externalities, and financing public spending. In addition, some tax rates may be institutionally fixed, several public expenditures may be contractually determined, etc. Within this context, i.e., within a second-best framework, quite a large set of instrument combinations is conceivable, indicating diverse efficiency implications, whereas the most efficient instruments are typically not available.

The task of the present work is to investigate the consequences of interjurisdictional competition under *imperfect* conditions. We analyse different policy regimes where local governments are limited to one or two tax rates. While we deny (free) availability of head taxes, we are concerned about distortionary taxation. Particular interest is focused on taxation of industrial capital and pollutant emissions. . This enables us not only to look at the provision of public services, but also to assess the environmental quality that prevails in equilibrium. To do this, we specify three different models. The first model (Chapter 2) investigates two different games of interjurisdictional competition where local governments provide public goods that benefit industry. In the first game, local governments' strategies are tax rates on mobile industrial capital; in the second, public expenditures. Although the literature suggests that competition in public expenditures is 'more competitive' than in tax rates, it turns out that in the case of industrial public goods this is not necessarily true. The reason is that capital taxation distorts the use of capital twofold, implying that a higher provision level of local public goods does not necessarily induce capital flight and may even attract capital. Moreover, we show that, in polar cases, public services may even be overprovided under both competition regimes.

The second approach (Chapter 3) considers interjurisdictional tax competition where local governments finance residential public goods through taxation of industrial pollutant emissions. Raising public funds in order to provide public services is one of the main reasons that prompt local governments to fix their equilibrium tax rates inefficiently. This creates a clear link between environmental quality and the supply of public services which is widely ignored in the literature. Contrary to what one might expect, it may occur that some governments determine their equilibrium emission taxes inefficiently high. However, the opposite is 'more likely'. Similarly, we show that, at least when regions are (sufficiently) identical,[4] governments face an incentive to deviate from intergovernmental cooperation by lowering their tax rates, implying that cooperative agreements are rather weak. This result gives some support to the hypothesis that interjurisdictional tax competition leads to 'ecological dumping'.

The third model, presented in Chapter 4, integrates interjurisdictional tax competition and environmental policy. Each local government supplies two public goods that benefit local industry and residents, respectively. Public expenditure is financed through distortionary taxation on industrial capital and pollutant emissions. In contrast to the traditional theory of tax competition, we find that overprovision of local public goods may emerge in equilibrium. Since emission taxes serve to finance public spending, the supply of public goods and the environmental quality are closely related. In the special case of a small region that cannot affect the national after-tax return to capital, we have the striking result that in equilibrium two different regimes can occur: either we have underprovision of public goods and an inefficiently high environmental quality, or we have overprovision of public goods and a too low environmental quality. These inefficiencies persevere as long as the federal government is not authorized to apply deliberate taxation-subsidy schemes. Correspondingly, unless regions are identical, we cannot hope to overcome the efficiency problem by symmetrical cooperative solutions.

NOTES

1. Note that the phrase *ecological dumping* – though it is widely used in the literature – is slightly inaccurate in this context. Dumping requires

price differentiation between the home and the foreign market. But what is meant by dumping here is that, due to relatively low environmental standards, one region gets a cost advantage for its exporting industry.

2. In Germany, the governments at all levels rely heavily on common shared taxes. In 1987, 76% of the tax receipts of the federal government stem from these taxes; for the Länder and the local governments the corresponding figures are 87% and 52% respectively of their tax revenues. (See Musgrave and Musgrave, 1990, p. 33.)

3. In 1984, the local governments (state governments) received about two-(one-)thirds of their revenues from grants. (See Musgrave and Musgrave, 1989, p. 23.)

4. Whenever we speak of *identical* regions, residents, consumers, firms etc., we mean economic units that cannot be distinguished with respect to the relevant characteristics.

2. Different Forms of Interjurisdictional Competition

1 INTRODUCTION

About ten years ago Zodrow and Mieszkowski (1986) set up a simple model of interjurisdictional tax competition. This work has been proven as a useful benchmark for the analysis of endogenous provision of local public goods in an interregional setting. Several models have been developed that could be viewed as deliberate extensions of the Zodrow and Mieszkowski (1986) approach. For example, Wilson (1985), section 6 and Burbidge and Myers (1994) introduce labour mobility. Tax instruments other than a source-based tax on capital income are investigated by Gordon (1986), Bucovetsky and Wilson (1991), and Hoyt (1991a). It has been well recognized that the outcome of interjurisdictional competition depends crucially on the number of competing regions (see Hoyt, 1991b). When their number becomes small,[1] strategic interactions between local governments play an important role. For the special case of two regions with immobile residents, Bucovetsky (1991) and Wilson (1991) investigate asymmetric tax competition between a small and a large region. In a multi-period setting, debt becomes, besides a capital tax rate, an available strategic policy tool. This instrument is analysed by Jensen and Toma (1991), considering a two-stage game of two regions. However, it has been overlooked for some time that, even in the simple setting where public goods are financed exclusively through a single tax rate, governments face two strategic variables, in principle: local governments can either fix independently their tax rates or their provision levels of public services. Accordingly, one may consider two different policy regimes: regions play either a game in tax rates or in public expenditures. Wildasin (1988) shows that, if local governments provide local public goods that benefit residents (so-called residential public goods), the equilibrium allocations of both games do not coincide, in general; more precisely, competition in public expenditures is more competitive than in tax rates, in the sense that in equilibrium each region's marginal rate of transformation (between the private and the public good) under expenditure competition is larger than under tax competition. The intuition behind this result is the following. While a Nash equilibrium in tax rates can be viewed as one with zero conjectural variations, an equilibrium in public expenditures corresponds to an equilibrium in tax rates with negative conjectural variations.[2]

These and many other extensions of the basic fiscal competition model are discussed in the literature. However, one aspect, though considered in the fundamental work of Zodrow and Mieszkowski (1986), is widely ignored: the provision of public goods that benefit industry (industrial public goods).[3] Empirically, the provision cost of industrial public services represents a significant part of public expenditure – particularly, of the public expenditures of lower level governments.[4] For example, in Germany the state governments (Länder) in 1992 spent 31.35%, or DM 106 659 million, of their total expenditures for public services that benefit, at least partly, industry.[5] (The corresponding figures for the local governments are 48%, or DM 103 324 million.)[6] Keeping this in mind, the neglect of endogenous provision of industrial public goods is, to say the least, inappropriate. One reason that the analysis of industrial public services plays a minor role in the economic literature might be that many authors expect both types of public goods to be (strategically) more or less equivalent. However, we should be careful in applying the results stemming from models of residential public goods to the case of industrial public goods. The reason is that industrial services which improve production possibilities promote economic activities. This, in turn, contrary to the case of residential public goods, affects residents' profit income (dividends) as well as public revenue. If more industrial public services attract more capital, public spending that favours industry induces a second-order effect on public revenue, i.e., revenue increases indirectly. Therefore, the welfare effects that result from the provision of industrial and residential public goods differ in size. This leads us to conclude that interjurisdictional competition where governments provide residential public goods differs significantly from the case where they provide industrial public goods. To prove this, we present a model of *imperfect* interjurisdictional competition, where local governments provide *industrial* public goods that are financed exclusively by capital taxation.

We show (i) that the equilibrium allocations of competition in capital tax rates and in public expenditures differ considerably from their residential counterparts, i.e., from the corresponding equilibria of those games where governments provide residential public goods, (ii) that competition in public expenditures is no longer necessarily 'more competitive' than competition in tax rates, and (iii) that it may occur that public services are overprovided in equilibrium.

The plan of this chapter is as follows. The next section sets up the model. In Section 3, two games of interjurisdictional competition are introduced: local governments compete either in tax rates or in expenditure levels. For both games, a region's best-reply curve is presented and contrasted with its optimal policy, where all policy tools are available. Since the analysis becomes rather arduous in the general case, we focus on identical regions and a symmetric equilibrium in Section 4. Both types of equilibria are contrasted with each other and our findings are illustrated by means of three examples. The last section summarizes the main results.

2 THE MODEL

We model a federal state that is composed of a small fixed number of jurisdictions, n.[7] Every local government provides a public good that benefits the resident firms (e.g., infrastructure) and is financed by taxation of mobile industrial capital, exclusively. Since no other sources of public funds are available, each local government can either fix independently its tax rate or its provision level of the public good and treats the other variable as the dependent one. Accordingly, we consider two different games (policy regimes): local governments compete either in tax rates or in public expenditures, i.e., their strategic variables are capital tax rates and public expenditures respectively. In any case, each government's objective is to maximize its residents' utility (pay-off function). To achieve this, each government acts strategically: while determining its strategic variable, the government anticipates the reactions of consumers and firms, but takes the behaviour of the other governments as given (reaction curve). The intersection of all n reaction curves gives us, depending on the mode of competition, either a Nash equilibrium in tax rates or in public expenditures.

On the production side local firms ignore their (potential) impact on prices and on the other agents' behaviour and behave perfectly competitively. More precisely, firms, while taking prices and the provision level of industrial public services as given, produce a homogeneous output good – the unique consumption good. For tractability, suppose that in each region there is only one firm,[8] implying that the number of firms equals n. Since our analysis focuses on taxation of industrial capital, all private inputs, except capital, are assumed to be fixed in production. In this case, we can write the production function of the firm residing in region j as a function of used capital, K^j, and the provision level of industrial public services, P^j, exclusively, $F^j(K^j, P^j) \ \forall j = 1, \ldots, n$. The production function F^j is assumed to be monotonously increasing in both variables with decreasing marginal products of capital, $F^j_{kk} < 0;$[9] in addition, the marginal product of capital is the higher, the more public services are provided, $F^j_{kp} > 0$. For any given values of the local price of capital and of the provision of public services, each firm maximizes its profits with respect to K^j. Using the private good as numéraire, each local firm's profits are given by

$$\Pi^j(K^j; P^j, p^j_k) \ = \ F^j(K^j, P^j) - K^j p^j_k \qquad \forall j = 1, \ldots, n,$$

where p^j_k denotes the after-tax price of capital in region j.

Let each region consist of identical, utility-maximizing, immobile[10] residents (homogeneous population). For analytical simplicity, we normalize the population of each region to unity, i.e., we assume that in each region there is only one inhabitant (or consumer).[11] Suppose that any local consumer's preferences can be represented by a monotonic, twice continuously differentiable, strictly concave utility function $\mathcal{U}^j(X^j)$, where X^j denotes her consumption level of the unique private good. Since the price of this item is normalized to unity, private expenditure is equal to X^j. Let each local resident hold all shares of the corresponding local firm, i.e., the consumer of region j receives the full profit of that firm residing in the same region, but she does not receive any income from outside firms.[12] In addition, she receives rent income from her portion, $\theta^j \in [0, 1]$, of the nationally fixed capital stock, $\bar{K}$, where $\sum_j \theta^j \equiv 1$. Denoting the nation-wide net return rate of capital by ρ, the private budget constraint of the consumer residing in region j is given by

$$X^j = F^j(K^j, P^j) - K^j p_k^j + \theta^j \rho \bar{K} \qquad \forall j. \qquad (2.1)$$

Assume that local governments are able to produce one unit of the public good by giving up one unit of the private good. Thus, since there is only one consumer, we may view the provision of local public goods as publicly supplied private goods.[13] Because the government is in effect able to transform public revenue into public services, the public budget constraint of region j, equating tax revenue and public spending, is given by

$$P^j = \tau^j K^j \qquad \forall j, \qquad (2.2)$$

where τ^j denotes the local government's tax rate levied on industrial capital, measured in units of the private good. Thus, $\tau^j K^j$ represents those units of the private good, collected from capital taxation, that serve to provide public goods.

Since we are dealing with a small number of regions, a variation of the local capital tax rate not only affects *local* capital demand but also the nation-wide allocation of capital. While, as indicated earlier, local governments do no act 'myopically' but strategically, each government recognizes that it has some impact on the equilibrium (pre-tax) price of capital. Realizing this, each local government can easily calculate the effect of any τ^j on the equilibrium value of ρ by taking into account the market-clearing condition for capital. For this purpose, we need to characterize the equilibrium of the capital market first.

Suppose that capital is interregionally freely mobile; and recall that firms behave perfectly competitively on all markets, implying that they take tax rates and the net price of capital as given. Thus, any profit-maximizing firm equates the value of the marginal product of capital and its after-tax price. Then, in any equilibrium of the capital market, the net return to capital, ρ, must be the same in all jurisdictions, i.e., we have

$$F_k^j(K^j, P^j) - \tau^j = \rho \qquad \forall j. \qquad (2.3)$$

Since in each region capital is paid by its marginal product, $F_k^j(K^j, P^j)$, resident j's dividend income[14] is equal to $F^j(K^j, P^j) - K^j F_k^j(K^j, P^j)$. Because capital supply is fixed by assumption, capital demand must exactly meet $\bar{K}$, in equilibrium,

$$\sum_{j=1}^{n} K^j(p_k^j, P^j) = \bar{K}, \qquad (2.4)$$

where $p_k^j := \rho + \tau^j$ denotes the local after-tax price of capital. Using the governmental budget constraints (2.2), the n equations given by (2.3) and the capital market-clearing condition, (2.4), determine simultaneously the equilibrium values of $K^1, \ldots, K^n$, and ρ.[15] Using these conditions, which characterize a *perfect* national capital market, each local government is able to compute its impact on the nation-wide net return to capital, $\partial \rho / \partial \tau^j$.[16]

3 TWO GAMES OF INTERJURISDICTIONAL COMPETITION

In this section, we compare the two games of interjurisdictional competition (and their resulting equilibria) where local governments use different strategic variables. Either governments engage in competition in tax rates or they compete in public expenditures. In the first case, governments' strategies are tax rates on mobile capital; in the second case, public expenditures.[17] Depending on the type of the strategic variable, two different equilibrium allocations emerge, in general.[18] To analyse and compare them (Section 4), we first have to derive any local government's reaction curve, that is, its best-reply curve for any given policy measures of the other governments.

Under any mode of interjurisdictional competition each government maximizes the utility of its resident (governmental pay-off function) with respect to its strategic variable. In doing this, it anticipates the behaviour of any local firm and the change of the net return to capital through taking into account firms' first-order conditions, (2.3), and the market-clearing condition for capital, (2.4). But before turning to the equilibrium behaviour of the local governments under both competition regimes, we characterize a single region's optimal allocation.

3.1 A Region's Optimal Allocation

As a benchmark, first we consider the (constrained) Pareto-efficient allocation of one region given the behaviour of the remainder of the nation. In other words, we investigate what is the best a single region can do given its initial endowment, $\theta^j \bar{K}$, and the chosen levels of the policy variables of the other governments. The optimal allocation of region j, defined in this sense, is derived by maximizing the resident's utility

$$\mathcal{U}\left(F^j(K^j, P^j) - K^j p_k^j + \theta^j \rho \bar{K} - P^j\right)$$

with respect to K^j and P^j directly[19] subject to the capital market-clearing condition (2.4). Then, the optimal allocation is characterized by[20]

$$F_p^j = 1, \tag{2.5}$$

$$F_k^j = \left(1 + \epsilon_K^j(\rho)\right)\rho - \theta^j \bar{K} \frac{\partial \rho}{\partial K^j}, \tag{2.6}$$

where $\frac{\partial \rho}{\partial K^j}$ denotes the marginal impact of local capital demand on the net return to capital, and $\epsilon_K^j(\rho) := \frac{\partial \rho}{\partial K^j} \frac{K^j}{\rho}$ denotes the corresponding elasticity (the elasticity of inverse capital demand).

Since the marginal rate of technical transformation between the private and the public good is equal to one, efficiency requires that the marginal product of public services in private production is also equal to one. This is guaranteed by condition (2.5). The local government should provide industrial services up to that point where their marginal product in the production process of the private good is equal to unity.

Condition (2.6) is the usual first-order condition for a monopsony corrected for an income term, $-\theta^j \bar{K} \partial \rho / \partial K^j$. The first term of the right hand side, the monopsony part, $(1 + \epsilon_K^j(\rho))\rho$, states that the marginal product of any input, namely capital, should be equal to one plus its elasticity of the inverse demand function times its factor price, $p_k = \rho$. The second term of the right hand side of (2.6) accounts for the income effect resulting from the resident's initial capital endowment. Since local capital demand has a positive impact on the national price of capital, one additional unit of capital used in local production increases the resident's interest income. This marginal income gain lowers the region's effective social price of capital – the right hand side of equation (2.6).

To obtain an alternative perspective, rewrite (2.6) as

$$F_k^j = \rho + \left(K^j - \theta^j \bar{K}\right) \frac{\partial \rho}{\partial K^j}. \tag{2.7}$$

The extent of local capital excess demand (or supply) plays a crucial role in determining the optimal use of capital. The distortion from the efficiency rule – marginal product of capital equal to factor price – increases with $|K^j - \theta^j \bar{K}|$. The more local capital demand exceeds its supply in absolute values, the more F_k differs from ρ. Hence, while the region's effective social price of capital differs from the efficient price, the optimal allocation is inefficient, in general. Only if local capital demand meets its local supply, $K^j = \theta^j \bar{K}$, or if local capital demand does not affect the nation-wide net return to capital, $\partial \rho / \partial K^j = 0$ (small region), is capital used at its efficient level. However, while $\partial \rho / \partial K^j > 0$, a capital net-exporting region uses capital beyond that point where its marginal product equals ρ. The reason is that additional capital demand drives up ρ and thereby the capital owner's income. The contrary is true for a net-importing region.

3.2   Competition in Tax Rates

Assume that each local government views its tax rate as the strategic variable, while it treats the provision level of public services, the left hand side of (2.2), as the dependent variable. Since each government believes that it cannot affect the tax rates of other, autonomous governments, it maximizes, for any given tax rates of the other governments, the utility of its resident with respect to the local tax rate on capital (reaction curve). In doing this, the government anticipates the behaviour of the local firm and the induced price change on the capital market. (Since we are dealing with a small number of regions, a variation of the local capital tax rate not only affects *local* capital demand but also the nation-wide allocation of capital.) In equilibrium, no local government is able to increase its resident's utility by changing the local tax rate, given the equilibrium tax rates of the other regions. The vector of these equilibrium tax rates defines the outcome of the game that we call *interjurisdictional competition in tax rates*.

Define the vector of local tax rates by $\vec{\tau} := (\tau^1, \ldots, \tau^n)^T$, and write the net return to capital as a function of this vector, $\rho(\vec{\tau})$. Since local capital demand depends on the local (gross) price of capital and on the provision level of local public services, the public and the private budget constraint respectively can be written as

$$P^j = \tau^j K^j \left(\tau^j + \rho(\vec{\tau}), P^j \right),$$ (2.8)

$$X^j = F^j \left(K^j \left(\tau^j + \rho(\vec{\tau}), P^j \right), P^j \right)$$
$$- K^j \left(\tau^j + \rho(\vec{\tau}), P^j \right) \left(\tau^j + \rho(\vec{\tau}) \right) + \theta^j \bar{K} \rho(\vec{\tau}).$$ (2.9)

Before characterizing a local government's equilibrium policy, we need to know how capital demand varies in response to a change of any local tax rate. Without loss of generality, assume that, at some given vector of tax rates, region j increases τ^j and adjusts its provision level appropriately. If this policy measure reduces local capital demand, dismissed capital has to allocate outside of the region, for the nation-wide supply of capital is assumed to be fixed. This influx of capital perceived by other regions causes their tax revenues to increase even though tax rates are held constant; and their provision levels change correspondingly. (The reverse is true if an increase of τ^j induces a capital movement towards region j, which may happen, as will soon become clear.) Thus, in either case, local governments create fiscal externalities[21] through their tax rates.[22]

To see how local capital demand varies if other governments do not respond in tax rates, totally differentiate local factor demand with respect to τ^j, yielding

$$\frac{\partial K^j}{\partial \tau^j} = K_1^j \left(1 + \frac{\partial \rho}{\partial \tau^j} \right) + K_2^j \frac{\partial P^j}{\partial \tau^j},$$ (2.10)

$$\frac{\partial K^i}{\partial \tau^j} = K_1^i \frac{\partial \rho}{\partial \tau^j} + K_2^i \frac{\partial P^i}{\partial \tau^j} \qquad \forall i \neq j,$$ (2.11)

where K_i^j denotes the partial derivative of local capital demand with respect to the i-th variable. Since each local government anticipates the extent of capital flight (or influx) which is triggered off by its policy, the sensitivity of capital demand with respect to local tax rates, characterized by (2.10) and (2.11), plays a crucial role in determining equilibrium policies.

While the utility of the resident of region j depends only on one variable, the optimization problem facing the government is simply to maximize its consumer's income subject to the equality between public revenue and expenditure. Therefore, differentiate the public and the private budget constraint, (2.8) and (2.9), with respect to τ^j. Using (2.10) and (2.11) gives us the change of the public good and of the private consumption good,

$$\frac{\partial P^j}{\partial \tau^j} = \frac{K^j + \tau^j K_1^j \left(1 + \frac{\partial \rho}{\partial \tau^j}\right)}{1 - \tau^j K_2^j}, \tag{2.12}$$

$$\frac{\partial X^j}{\partial \tau^j} = -K^j \left(1 + \frac{\partial \rho}{\partial \tau^j}\right) + F_p^j \frac{\partial P^j}{\partial \tau^j} + \theta^j \bar{K} \frac{\partial \rho}{\partial \tau^j}. \tag{2.13}$$

Analogously, differentiating the public and the private budget constraint of region i yields the marginal external effects induced by tightening the tax screw in region j,

$$\frac{\partial P^i}{\partial \tau^j} = \frac{\tau^i K_1^i \frac{\partial \rho}{\partial \tau^j}}{1 - \tau^i K_2^i} \qquad \forall i \neq j, \tag{2.14}$$

$$\frac{\partial X^i}{\partial \tau^j} = -K^i \frac{\partial \rho}{\partial \tau^j} + F_p^i \frac{\partial P^i}{\partial \tau^j} + \theta^i \bar{K} \frac{\partial \rho}{\partial \tau^j} \qquad \forall i \neq j. \tag{2.15}$$

The change of any resident's consumption, (2.13) and (2.15), consists of three additive terms. The first two terms reflect her change in dividend income stemming from the public policy's impact on the profit of the local firm: an increase of the local tax rate raises the cost of the residing firm, whereas the accompanying change of public services benefits production. The third term takes into account the effect on interest income caused by the influence of the local tax rate on the nation-wide net return to capital.

Substituting (2.12) into (2.13), setting the right hand side of (2.13) equal to zero, and dividing the result by (2.12) yields the first-order condition of the optimization problem of the local government:

$$-\frac{\partial X^j / \partial \tau^j}{\partial P^j / \partial \tau^j} = \frac{K^j + \frac{\partial \rho}{\partial \tau^j} \left(K^j - \theta^j \bar{K}\right)}{K^j + \left(1 + \frac{\partial \rho}{\partial \tau^j}\right) \tau^j K_1^j} \left(1 - \tau^j K_2^j\right) - F_p^j \stackrel{!}{=} 0. \tag{2.16}$$

Condition (2.16) states that the local government should adjust its tax rate such that the marginal provision cost of the public good net of its marginal benefit equals zero. In other words, the social marginal rate of transformation between the private and the public good should be equal to the marginal product of public services in private production.

Note that because we consider the provision of industrial rather than residential public goods, taxation rule (2.16) differs significantly from the one derived by Wildasin (1988), equation (8.1) therein.[23] Apparently, both formulae differ by two terms. Firstly, the conventional term determining the marginal rate of transformation (respectively substitution), the fraction term, is multiplied by $(1 - \tau^j K_2^j)$; and secondly, the marginal rate of transformation should be equal to F_p^j. This confirms our claim that, under tax competition, the equilibrium allocations differ significantly if we consider either residential or industrial public goods. (And the same is true under expenditure competition.) Let us go briefly through the single terms of the right hand side of equation (2.16).

The fraction term accounts for those units of the private good that have to be sacrificed to raise public revenue, sufficient to provide one additional unit of industrial public services. The numerator represents the marginal impact of τ^j on private consumption: for a fixed provision level of the public good, a marginal increase of τ^j reduces the resident's profit income (dividends) by $K^j + \frac{\partial \rho}{\partial \tau^j} K^j$ and her rent income by $-\frac{\partial \rho}{\partial \tau^j} \theta^j \bar{K}$. The denominator represents the marginal impact of τ^j on public revenue, given the provision level of the public good. Thus, we may interpret this fraction as the marginal rate of transformation between private income and public funds for a given provision level of public services. Roughly speaking, this term reflects the social marginal value of income using governmental income as numéraire.

Now consider the additional factor that stems from the fact that we deal with industrial public goods, $(1 - \tau^j K_2^j)$. If K_2^j is positive, this bracket term is smaller than one. In this case, since the provision of the public good becomes less expensive, its supply is extended. The reason is that the provision of industrial services attracts, *ceteris paribus*, additional capital, broadening the tax basis of capital taxation. This effect reduces the provision cost of industrial public goods encouraging their provision. We call this indirect effect the *fiscal 'feed-back effect'* of industrial public goods. Since the bracket term $(1 - \tau^j K_2^j)$ measures the (effective) marginal cost of industrial public services, the first part of (2.16) represents the social value of the provision cost of one additional unit of the industrial public good (or the social marginal rate of transformation between the private and the public good).

Since public services improve the production technology of the private sector, the marginal rate of transformation should be equal to F_p^j. Note that residents do not benefit directly from the provision of industrial public services. Therefore, the impact of P^j on the production function, F^j, already represents the total marginal social benefit that accrues from the provision of the public good.

Evidently, the local government's first-order condition, given by (2.16), and the region's optimality rule, given by (2.6) and (2.5), do not coincide, in general. This divergence shows that the local regulator is not able (or not willing) to pursue the region's optimal policy by means of a single tax rate on capital. While the industrial public good is not provided at that level where its marginal product, F_p^j, is equal to one (the technical marginal rate of transformation of the public sector), it is provided inefficiently. Namely, if in equation (2.16) F_p^j is greater (smaller) than one, public services are underprovided (overprovided).

To gain further insight into the capital market, we calculate a local government's impact on the net return to capital, $\partial \rho / \partial \tau^j$. Differentiating the market-clearing condition, (2.4), with respect to τ^j yields

$$\sum_{i \neq j} \left(K_1^i \frac{\partial \rho}{\partial \tau^j} + K_2^i \frac{\partial P^i}{\partial \tau^j} \right) + K_1^j \left(1 + \frac{\partial \rho}{\partial \tau^j} \right) + K_2^j \frac{\partial P^j}{\partial \tau^j} = 0.$$

Using (2.12) and (2.14) and solving for $\partial \rho / \partial \tau^j$ gives

$$\frac{\partial \rho}{\partial \tau^j} = -\frac{\dfrac{K_1^j}{1 - \tau^j K_2^j}}{\displaystyle\sum_{i=1}^n \dfrac{K_1^i}{1 - \tau^i K_2^i}} - \frac{\dfrac{K_2^j K^j}{1 - \tau^j K_2^j}}{\displaystyle\sum_{i=1}^n \dfrac{K_1^i}{1 - \tau^i K_2^i}}. \tag{2.17}$$

To evaluate (2.17), we need the following lemma.[24]

Lemma 2.1 *Capital demand falls if, ceteris paribus, the gross price of capital increases; it rises if, ceteris paribus, the provision of public services increases:*

$$K_1^j = \frac{1}{F_{kk}^j} < 0, \tag{2.18}$$

$$K_2^j = -\frac{F_{kp}^j}{F_{kk}^j} > 0. \tag{2.19}$$

Proof: Differentiate firm j's first-order condition, $F_k^j(K^j, P^j) = p_k^j$, with respect to p_k^j and P^j, holding P^j and p_k^j constant. Using the concavity of F^j and $F_{kp}^j > 0$, this procedure proves Lemma 2.1. $\qquad\square$

Since K_2^j is positive by Lemma 2.1, the only term whose sign is still ambiguous is $1 - \tau^j K_2^j$. While the sign of this term depends on the curvature of the production function, it can be either positive or negative. Defining $\varepsilon_{Pj}^j := P^j K_2^j / K^j$ as the elasticity of capital demand with respect to the provision level of public services, we can use the following condition as a benchmark of distinction.[25]

Condition 2.1 *Evaluated in some suitable neighbourhood of an equilibrium in tax rates, the elasticity of capital demand with respect to the provision level of public services satisfies*

$$\varepsilon_{Pj}^j < 1.$$

Using Condition (2.1), we directly have the following lemma, enabling us to determine the sign of $1 - \tau^j K_2^j$.

Lemma 2.2 *The effective marginal cost of industrial public services is positive,*

$$1 - \tau^j K_2^j > 0,$$

if, and only if, Condition 2.1 holds.

Proof: Follows from Condition 2.1. □

By Lemma 2.2, the 'feed-back effect' is not too large in the sense that the effective marginal cost of industrial public services becomes negative if Condition 2.1 holds.

Using Lemma 2.2, Condition 2.1 provides us with our first proposition.

Proposition 2.1 *Under Condition 2.1, regions' average impact on the net return to capital is larger than* $-1/n$.

Proof: Define $\delta^j := - \left(\frac{K_2^j K^j}{1 - \tau^j K_2^j} \right) \left(\sum_{i=1}^n \frac{K_1^i}{1 - \tau^i K_2^i} \right)^{-1}$. Since $K_2^j > 0$ and $1 - \tau^j K_2^j > 0$ by Lemma 2.2, δ^j is positive for all j. Summing (2.17) over all j and dividing by n yields

$$\overline{\frac{\partial \rho}{\partial \tau}} := \frac{1}{n} \sum_{j=1}^n \frac{\partial \rho}{\partial \tau^j} = -\frac{1}{n} + \bar{\delta} > -\frac{1}{n},$$

where $\bar{\delta} := \frac{1}{n} \sum_{i=1}^n \delta^j > 0$. □

Proposition 2.1 states that, contrary to the standard model of interjurisdictional competition in tax rates, $\partial \rho / \partial \tau^j \in (-1, 0)$ is not necessarily true.[26] More precisely, for any local government's impact on the

nation-wide net return to capital we have $\partial \rho / \partial \tau^j \in (-1 + \delta^j, \delta^j)$. If
local governments provide *industrial* public goods, their impact on the
nation-wide net return to capital is higher (smaller in absolute values if
$\partial \rho / \tau^j$ is negative) than in the case where local governments provide *residential* public goods. The reason is that capital taxation not only drives
out capital but improves the production possibilities and thus attracts
new capital. Since the revenue from capital taxation is spent in favour of
the industry, the extent of capital flight is reduced ('feed-back effect').
Therefore, the marginal impact of the local tax rate on ρ is larger, i.e.,
less negative, if governments provide industrial public goods.

Note that the impact of the local tax rate on the net return to capital
may even be positive. Since $\partial \rho / \partial \tau^j$ may lie in $(0, \delta^j)$, we cannot exclude
the possibility that enhancing the provision of public goods increases lo-
cal capital demand. From the literature we know that this typically does
not occur if governments provide residential public goods.[27] If, however,
firms benefit from public services, a higher provision level might attract
capital by more than a higher tax rate deters it. In this case, the 'feed-
back effect' is so strong that local capital demand is increased, possibly
resulting in a higher net return to capital. Of course, the concrete sign of
$\partial \rho / \partial \tau^j$ depends on the elasticities of capital demand in *all* regions. Let
$\varepsilon^j_{\rho+\tau^j} := (\rho + \tau^j) K_1^j / K^j$ denote the elasticity of capital demand with
respect to the (after-tax) price of capital. We use the following condition
as a distinctive mark.

Condition 2.2 *Evaluated in some suitable neighbourhood of an equilibrium, capital demand satisfies*

$$-\varepsilon^j_{\rho+\tau^j} \frac{\tau^j}{\rho + \tau^j} > \varepsilon^j_{P^j}.$$

Using Condition (2.2), we can state the following lemma, which helps us
to determine the sign of $\partial \rho / \partial \tau^j$.

Lemma 2.3 *In capital demand, the price effect dominates the provision
effect of the public good, in the sense that*

$$K_1^j + K_2^j K^j < 0,$$

if, and only if, Condition 2.2 holds.

Proof: Follows from Condition 2.2.   □

Evaluating equation (2.17) under Condition 2.2 gives us a unique sign of $\partial \rho / \partial \tau^j$.

Proposition 2.2 *Let Condition 2.1 either hold or not hold for all regions, simultaneously. The nation-wide net return to capital, ρ, depends negatively (positively) on the local tax rate on capital, τ^j, if, and only if, Condition 2.2 holds (does not hold).*

Proof: By definition of $\varepsilon_{\rho+\tau^j}^j$ and $\varepsilon_{\rho^j}^j$, Condition 2.2 is equivalent to $K_1^j + K_2^j K^j < 0$. Rewriting (2.17) as

$$\frac{\partial \rho}{\partial \tau^j} = -\left(1 + K^j \frac{K_2^j}{K_1^j}\right) \frac{\dfrac{K_1^j}{1 - \tau^j K_2^j}}{\sum_{i=1}^n \dfrac{K_1^i}{1 - \tau^i K_2^i}}$$

proves our claim. □

Note that Condition 2.2 is equivalent to $F_{kp}^j < 1/K^j$, while Condition 2.1 is equivalent to $F_{kp}^j < -F_{kk}^j/\tau^j$. Therefore, there may exist some range where Condition 2.1 is fulfilled but Condition 2.2 is violated: $0 < 1/K^j < F_{kp}^j < -F_{kk}^j/\tau^j$, respectively where Condition 2.2 holds but Condition 2.1 does not: $0 < -F_{kk}^j/\tau^j < F_{kp}^j < 1/K^j$. Thus, although it seems to be quite convincing to presume that Conditions 2.1 and 2.2 hold, equilibria are conceivable where either one or both of them do not hold. Accordingly, in analysing the outcome of interjurisdictional competition in tax rates, we consider four distinct cases characterized by the (in-)validity of Conditions 2.1 and 2.2 below.[28]

Before turning to the competition regime where, instead of setting tax rates, local governments determine public expenditures directly, we wish to consider the special case of a single region. If the whole nation consists of just one jurisdiction ($n = 1$ and $\theta = 1$), K is equal to $\bar{K}$, for 'local' capital demand must meet 'local' capital supply. Moreover, from (2.17) we have

$$\frac{\partial \rho}{\partial \tau} = -\left(1 + K \frac{K_2}{K_1}\right).$$

Substituting this into (2.16) gives us the first-order condition for the single government,

$$\frac{K(1 - \tau K_2)}{K + \tau K_1 - \tau(K_1 + K K_2)} = 1 \overset{!}{=} F_p.$$

As we would expect, for $n = 1$, public goods are provided efficiently. If the whole nation consists only of one region, all induced effects from capital movement are internalized. The reason is that capital has no opportunity to avoid a higher tax rate, i.e., the government need not be afraid of capital flight. (See, e.g., Hoyt, 1991b.) In this case, capital taxation is in effect non-distortionary.

3.3 Competition in Public Expenditures

Let us now consider the case where local governments compete in public expenditures. In this case, their strategic variables are the P^js. Each local government determines its level of public expenditure, i.e., its provision level of public goods, given the (equilibrium) provision levels of the other regions. From the equilibrium levels of public services it is possible to derive the capital tax rates that cover exactly the provision cost (expenditure).

Let $\vec{P} := (P^1, \ldots, P^n)^T$ denote the vector of provision levels of local public goods. While local governments compete in public services, not in tax rates, the public budget constraint of region j, previously given by (2.8), now takes the form

$$P^j = \tau^j(\vec{P}) \, K^j \left(\tau^j(\vec{P}) + \rho(\vec{\tau}(\vec{P})), P^j \right). \tag{2.20}$$

Differentiating the corresponding private budget constraint

$$\begin{aligned}
X^j = {} & F^j \left(K^j \left(\tau^j(\vec{P}) + \rho(\vec{\tau}(\vec{P})), P^j \right), P^j \right) + \theta^j \bar{K} \rho(\vec{\tau}(\vec{P})) \\
& - K^j \left(\tau^j(\vec{P}) + \rho(\vec{\tau}(\vec{P})), P^j \right) \left[\tau^j + \rho(\vec{\tau}(\vec{P})) \right]
\end{aligned} \tag{2.21}$$

with respect to P^j yields the social marginal rate of transformation between the private and the public good net of its marginal product in private production,

$$-\frac{\partial X^j}{\partial P^j} = -F_p^j + K^j \frac{\partial \tau^j}{\partial P^j} + \left(K^j - \theta^j \bar{K} \right) \frac{d\rho}{d\vec{\tau}} \cdot \frac{\partial \vec{\tau}}{\partial P^j}, \tag{2.22}$$

where we have used the following notation: $\frac{d\rho}{d\vec{\tau}} := \left(\frac{\partial \rho}{\partial \tau^1}, \ldots, \frac{\partial \rho}{\partial \tau^n} \right)$ denotes the gradient (vector) of ρ; and $\frac{\partial \vec{\tau}}{\partial P^j} := \left(\frac{\partial \tau^i}{\partial P^j} \right)_{i=1,\ldots,n}$, the jth column of the Jacobian matrix of $\vec{\tau}$. A '$\cdot$' indicates the inner product. Setting the right hand side equal to zero determines implicitly the provision level of public services in region j.

To evaluate (2.22), we have to calculate the vectors $d\rho/d\vec{\tau}$ and $\partial\vec{\tau}/\partial P^j$. Since the components of $d\rho/d\vec{\tau}$ are given by (2.17), it remains to calculate $\partial\tau^j/\partial P^j$ and $\partial\tau^i/\partial P^j$ $\forall i \neq j$. Differentiating the public budget constraint, (2.20), with respect to P^j yields a system of n equations that must be solved for the n unknown derivatives. Using $\frac{dK^j}{dP^j} = \frac{\partial K^j}{\partial P^j} + \frac{dK^j}{d\vec{\tau}} \cdot \frac{\partial \vec{\tau}}{\partial P^j}$, where the components of the gradient $\frac{dK^j}{d\vec{\tau}}$ are given by (2.10) and (2.11), this procedure yields

$$\frac{\partial\tau^j}{\partial P^j}\left[K^j + \tau^j K_1^j\left(1 + \frac{\partial\rho}{\partial\tau^j}\right)\right] + \tau^j K_1^j \sum_{l\neq j}\frac{\partial\rho}{\partial\tau^l}\frac{\partial\tau^l}{\partial P^j} + \tau^j K_2^j = 1, \quad (2.23)$$

$$\frac{\partial\tau^i}{\partial P^j}\left[K^i + \tau^i K_1^i\left(1 + \frac{\partial\rho}{\partial\tau^i}\right)\right]$$
$$+ \tau^i K_1^i \sum_{\substack{l\neq j \\ l\neq i}}\frac{\partial\rho}{\partial\tau^l}\frac{\partial\tau^l}{\partial P^j} + \tau^i K_1^i \frac{\partial\rho}{\partial\tau^j}\frac{\partial\tau^j}{\partial P^j} = 0. \quad (2.24)$$

Assuming weak symmetry, in the sense that $\partial\rho/\partial\tau^i = \partial\rho/\partial\tau^j$ $\forall i, j$ and $\partial\tau^i/\partial P^j = \partial\tau^l/\partial P^j$ $\forall i, l \neq j$, we can solve (2.24) for $\partial\tau^i/\partial P^j$,

$$\frac{\partial\tau^i}{\partial P^j} = -\frac{\tau^i K_1^i \frac{\partial\rho}{\partial\tau^j}\frac{\partial\tau^j}{\partial P^j}}{K^i + \tau^i K_1^i\left(1 + \frac{\partial\rho}{\partial\tau^i}\right) + (n-2)\tau^i K_1^i \frac{\partial\rho}{\partial\tau^i}}. \quad (2.25)$$

Substituting this result into (2.23) yields

$$\frac{\partial\tau^j}{\partial P^j} = \frac{\Delta_i\left(1 - \tau^j K_2^j\right)}{\Delta_i\left(K^j + \tau^j K_1^j\left(1 + \frac{\partial\rho}{\partial\tau^j}\right)\right) - (n-1)\tau^j\tau^i K_1^j K_1^i \frac{\partial\rho}{\partial\tau^j}\frac{\partial\rho}{\partial\tau^i}}, \quad (2.26)$$

where

$$\Delta_i := K^i + \tau^i K_1^i\left(1 + \frac{\partial\rho}{\partial\tau^i}\right) + (n-2)\tau^i K_1^i \frac{\partial\rho}{\partial\tau^i}.$$

Resubstituting (2.26) into (2.25) gives $\partial\tau^i/\partial P^j$. Using these results we can, at least in principle, compute any local government's equilibrium provision level. Unfortunately, the formulae become rather inconvenient and calculations are tedious. To gain further insight, we make some simplifying assumptions in the subsequent analysis. For the moment, all we can say is that the tax and the expenditure equilibrium allocation do

not coincide, in general. Only if, evaluated at the corresponding equilibrium variables, (2.16) and (2.22) hold simultaneously, do both allocations
coincide. However, there is no inherent reason to expect this.[29]

4   IDENTICAL JURISDICTIONS

To allow for a comparison of the equilibrium policies under the different competition regimes, it is instructive to consider the special case of
identical jurisdictions. To achieve this, we first have to investigate the
particular impact of any local government on the capital market in either
regime. Knowing the paths of capital demands and the nation-wide net
return to capital, we can derive the marginal rates of transformation in
both cases and compare the corresponding equilibrium taxation rules.[30]
This comparison allows us to judge which regime leads to 'more competitive' behaviour and whether overprovision of public goods possibly
occurs.

4.1   Competition in Tax Rates

First of all, note that in the special case of identical regions, we have
$\theta^j = 1/n \ \forall j$; and since in each jurisdiction, equilibrium local capital
demand must exactly meet local capital supply, it must be true that
$K^j = \theta^j \bar{K} \ \forall j$. Using this, a local government's impact on ρ reduces to

$$\frac{\partial \rho}{\partial \tau^j} = -\frac{1}{n}\left(1 + K^j \frac{K^j_2}{K^j_1}\right) \qquad \forall j. \qquad (2.27)$$

Even under the simplifying assumption of identical regions, we are not
able to determine unambiguously the sign of $\partial \rho / \partial \tau^j$, in general. It still
depends on Condition 2.2, and we cannot be more precise than in Propo-
sition 2.2.

Using $F^j_{kp} > 0$, we have that, under Condition 2.2, an increase of τ^j
causes the pre-tax and the after-tax price of capital to move in opposite
directions; if, however, Condition 2.2 does not hold, they move in the
same direction, i.e., both prices increase.

Lemma 2.4 *The after-tax price of capital in region j, p^j_k, rises if the
capital tax rate of region j, τ^j, is increased.*

Proof: Using (2.27), $1+\frac{\partial \rho}{\partial \tau^j}$ is equal to $\frac{n-1}{n}-\frac{K^j}{n}\frac{K^j_2}{K^j_1}$. Since K^j_2 is positive, this term is also positive (for all $n > 1$). $\square$

According to Lemma 2.4, an increase of τ^j leads to a higher after-tax price of capital in region j; and by inspecting equation (2.27), we see that an increase of a local tax rate has a negative impact on the nation-wide net return to capital if, and only if, Condition 2.2 is fulfilled.

So far, we have analysed how ρ and p^j_k respond to changes of τ^j. But we are actually more interested in the variations of capital demand. Namely, a fundamental question is, does capital taxation induce capital flight or possibly an influx of capital? To see how capital demand changes, substitute $\partial P^j/\partial \tau^j = \tau^j\,\partial K^j/\partial \tau^j + K^j$ into (2.10), yielding

$$\frac{\partial K^j}{\partial \tau^j} = \frac{K^j_1\left(1+\frac{\partial \rho}{\partial \tau^j}\right)+K^j_2 K^j}{1-\tau^j K^j_2} = \frac{n-1}{n}\frac{K^j_1 + K^j_2 K^j}{1-\tau^j K^j_2},$$

where we have made use of (2.27) for the last equality. We see that, under Condition 2.1, $\partial K^j/\partial \tau^j$ being positive is equivalent to $K^j_1 + K^j_2 K^j > 0$. This gives us the next proposition.

Proposition 2.3 *If a local government increases its tax rate on capital, local capital demand decreases if, and only if,*

- *either Conditions 2.1 and 2.2 hold*

- *or Conditions 2.1 and 2.2 do not hold*

simultaneously.

If, however, one condition is fulfilled while the other is violated, $\partial K^j/\partial \tau^j$ is positive. Compounding Proposition 2.2 and Proposition 2.3, we see that, in general, four distinct cases may emerge:

Case 1: Under Conditions 2.1 and 2.2, the elasticity of capital demand with respect to the provision level of public services is low: $\varepsilon^j_{P^j} < \min\left\{1, -\varepsilon^j_{\rho+\tau^j}\tau^j/(\rho+\tau^j)\right\}$. Accordingly, a rise of the local tax rate induces capital flight and consequently higher capital demand and provision levels in the other regions. Clearly, while K^j decreases but P^j increases,[31] the marginal product of capital in region j goes up. However, to determine the effect on the nation-wide net return to capital, we have to consider the change of the marginal product of capital in the other regions. Since $\partial F_k^i / \partial \tau^j = \partial \rho / \partial \tau^j \,\forall i \neq j$, it is the change of the marginal product in the other regions that determines the effect on ρ. By Condition 2.2, ρ falls and so does F_k^i for all $i \neq j$. (The negative impact of a higher employment level of capital on its marginal product outweighs the positive impact of a higher P^i on F_k^i.) Thus, capital owners of all regions suffer from a rise of τ^j: those who invest in region j suffer since the higher marginal product of capital is taxed away – recall that by Lemma 2.4 the after-tax price of capital increases; while those who invest elsewhere endure a loss from the influx of capital, resulting in a lower net return to capital. This is the standard result which we know from the traditional theory of interjurisdictional competition.

Case 2: If Condition 2.1 holds but 2.2 does not, the elasticity of capital demand with respect to the provision level of public services is relatively low, $\varepsilon_{Pj}^j < 1$; yet, it is sufficiently high to dominate the price effect, $\varepsilon_{Pj}^j > -\varepsilon_{\rho+\tau j}^j \tau^j / (\rho + \tau^j)$. Thus, increasing public services leads to higher local capital demand in region j (and also to a higher marginal product of capital even though capital is taxed more severely). The resulting fall of K^i and P^i for all $i \neq j$, results in a rise of F_k^i. (The positive effect of a higher employment level of capital on its marginal product exceeds the negative effect resulting from a lower level of public services on F_k^i.) Therefore, the extension of provision of public services in region j triggers an inflow of capital into this region and an overall net return to capital. That is, capital owners of all regions gain from a higher tax τ^j.

Case 3: If Condition 2.1 is violated but 2.2 holds, the marginal impact of P^j on F_k^j is not sufficiently high to dominate the price effect, $\varepsilon_{Pj}^j < -\varepsilon_{\rho+\tau j}^j \tau^j / (\rho + \tau^j)$, although $\varepsilon_{Pj}^j 1$ exceeds unity. Again, an increase of τ^j and P^j causes an inflow of capital and augments F_k^j; while, on the other hand, it decreases K^i and P^i. But, contrary to Case 2, the compound effect on F_k^i is negative. This is because the marginal decrease of P^i outweighs the positive impact of a lower K^i on F_k^i. However, a fall of $F_k^i \,\forall i \neq j$ is equivalent to $\partial \rho / \partial \tau^j < 0$.

Case 4: In this case, both conditions do not hold, implying that the elasticity of capital demand with respect to the provision level of public services is the highest: $\varepsilon^j_{Pj} > \max\left\{1, -\varepsilon^j_{\rho+\tau^j}\tau^j/(\rho+\tau^j)\right\}$. However, the induced rise of ρ, accompanied by a higher tax τ^j, leads to lower capital demand in region j and to an inflow of capital in all other regions. In these regions, the effect of a higher provision level of public services dominates the effect of a higher employment level of capital on F^i_k; hence, the marginal product of capital increases in all regions.

Thus, contrary to the traditional tax competition literature, where public services benefit consumers, not firms, taxation of industrial capital *may* attract new capital if either

$$-\varepsilon^j_{\rho+\tau^j}\frac{\tau^j}{\rho+\tau^j} < \varepsilon^j_{Pj} < 1 \quad \text{or} \quad 1 < \varepsilon^j_{Pj} < -\varepsilon^j_{\rho+\tau^j}\frac{\tau^j}{\rho+\tau^j}.$$

Thus, if the elasticity of capital demand with respect to its own price is either sufficiently low or high (Cases 2 and 3), there is some scope for an influx of capital.

Now let us investigate a local government's equilibrium policy in more detail. If local governments engage in tax competition, each region's equilibrium policy is determined by equation (2.16). Taking $\theta^j = 1/n$ and the requirement of a symmetric equilibrium $K^j = \theta^j \bar{K}$ into account, and substituting (2.17) into (2.16), government j's first-order condition reduces to

$$\frac{K^j\left(1 - \tau^j K^j_2\right)}{K^j + \tau^j K^j_1\left(1 + \dfrac{\partial\rho}{\partial\tau^j}\right)} = F^j_p, \tag{2.28}$$

or equivalently to

$$\frac{K^j\left(1 - \tau^j K^j_2\right)}{K^j\left(1 - \tau^j K^j_2\right) - (n-1)\tau^j K^j_1\dfrac{\partial\rho}{\partial\tau^j}} = F^j_p. \tag{2.29}$$

Provided that $1 - \tau^j K^j_2 > 0$, we see from (2.29) that the marginal rate of transformation between the private and the public good is greater than unity if $(n-1)\partial\rho/\partial\tau^j$ is negative. Using (2.27), this is equivalent to $K^j_1 + K^j_2 K^j < 0$. However, if Condition 2.1 does not hold, and thus $1 - \tau^j K^j_2$ is negative by Lemma 2.2, public services are underprovided if Condition 2.2 is not fulfilled either.

Proposition 2.4 *Let local governments of identical regions (with $n \geq 2$) engage in competition in tax rates on capital. Public services are underprovided if, and only if,*

- *either Conditions 2.1 and 2.2 hold*

- *or both of them do not hold.*

Correspondingly, public services are overprovided if, and only if, one of these conditions is fulfilled while the other is not.

Assume for a moment that Condition 2.1 is fulfilled. Since the crucial term determining the provision level of public goods, $K_1^j + K_2^j K^j$, also determines $\partial \rho / \partial \tau^j$ (see equation (2.27)), we can reformulate Proposition 2.4 as follows. Provided that Condition 2.1 holds, local public goods are underprovided (overprovided) if, and only if, $\partial \rho / \partial \tau^j$ is negative (positive). In the 'standard' case of interjurisdictional competition where $\partial \rho / \partial \tau^j < 0$, industrial public services are underprovided. If, however, Condition 2.1 does not hold, we have overprovision under Condition 2.2. In other words, public services are underprovided in Cases 1 and 4, but overprovided in Cases 2 and 3. Recalling Proposition 2.3, we see that there is a direct link between capital flight and the provision level of public goods: local public goods are underprovided (overprovided) if, and only if, a higher tax rate induces an outflow (influx) of capital.

Independent of Condition 2.1, public goods are provided efficiently if the elasticity of capital demand with respect to the public good is equal to minus the elasticity with respect to the gross price of capital times the percentage tax rate on capital (based on its gross price):

$$\varepsilon_P^j = -\frac{\tau^j}{\rho + \tau^j} \varepsilon_{\rho + \tau}^j. \tag{2.30}$$

In this case, the local government has, at the margin, no impact on the nation-wide net return to capital, implying that strategic effects cancel out.

The important feature of Proposition 2.4 is that, in the case of identical regions, overprovision as well as efficient provision of local public goods *may* occur.[32] Clearly, the 'probability' of efficiency as equilibrium outcome is rather low, for there is no reason to expect that (2.30) is fulfilled; rather (2.30) will only be satisfied by chance.[33] Yet, the examples given below will show that overprovision of public goods may, in fact, occur.

Moreover, recalling Proposition 2.3, we see that Proposition 2.4 gives us a direct link between capital flight and the provision level of public goods: local public goods are underprovided (overprovided) if, and only if, a higher tax rate induces an outflow (influx) of capital; i.e., public services are underprovided in Cases 1 and 4, but overprovided in Cases 2 and 3.

This finding is new and contrasts with the standard result of the traditional theory of interjurisdictional competition dealing with provision of *residential* public goods: If local governments provide public goods that benefit residents, their provision levels are too low at a symmetric equilibrium of identical regions. Moreover, in the traditional literature, even for heterogeneous jurisdictions local residential public goods are underprovided unless local capital excess demand is 'too high'. In the case of industrial public goods, however, efficient provision and overprovision of local public goods may emerge in equilibrium; namely, the latter occurs if either Condition 2.1 or 2.2 (but not both) does not hold.

4.2 Competition in Public Expenditures

Next consider interjurisdictional competition in public expenditures. Recall that in this case the government's independent variable is the provision level of the public good, while the tax rate is a dependent variable. Again, focusing on a symmetric Nash equilibrium, the necessary change of the local tax rate to increase the provision level of the public by one unit is given by

$$\frac{\partial \tau^j}{\partial P^j} = \frac{\left(K^j + \tau^j K_1^j + (n-1)\tau^j K_1^j \frac{\partial \rho}{\partial \tau^j}\right)}{\left(K^j + \tau^j K_1^j + (n-1)\tau^j K_1^j \frac{\partial \rho}{\partial \tau^j}\right)} \times$$

$$\frac{\left(1 - \tau^j K_2^j\right)}{\left(K^j + \tau^j K_1^j \left(1 + \frac{\partial \rho}{\partial \tau^j}\right)\right) - (n-1)\left(\tau^j K_1^j \frac{\partial \rho}{\partial \tau^j}\right)^2}.$$

Using (2.27), this simplifies further to

$$\frac{\partial \tau^j}{\partial P^j} = \frac{nK^j + \tau^j K_1^j + \tau^j K_2^j K^j - n\tau^j K_2^j K^j}{nK^j \left(K^j + \tau^j K_1^j\right)}. \tag{2.31}$$

Substituting (2.31) into (2.25) and using $\tau^i = \tau^j \; \forall i, j$, gives

$$\frac{\partial \tau^i}{\partial P^j} = \frac{\tau^j \left(K_1^j + K_2^j K^j \right)}{n K^j \left(K^j + \tau^j K_1^j \right)} \qquad \forall i \neq j. \tag{2.32}$$

Equations (2.31) and (2.32) allow us to calculate region j's marginal impact on the nation-wide net return to capital,

$$\frac{\partial \rho}{\partial P^j} = \frac{d\rho}{d\bar{\tau}} \cdot \frac{\partial \bar{\tau}}{\partial P^j} = -\frac{1}{n} \frac{K_1^j + K_2^j K^j}{K^j K_1^j}. \tag{2.33}$$

The effect of P^j on ρ equals $\partial \rho / \partial \tau^j$ divided by K^j. Thus, similar to what we found in the case of tax competition, the sign of a local government's impact on the nation-wide net return to capital depends on Condition 2.2.

Remark: Observe that in the case of identical regions, the local tax rate, τ^j, is linear homogeneous in the vector of local provision levels, $\vec{P}$. To see this, multiply $\partial \tau^j / \partial P^i$ by P^i and sum over all $i = 1, \ldots, n$. Using (2.31) and (2.32), this procedure yields

$$\sum_{i=1}^{n} \frac{\partial \tau^j(\vec{P})}{\partial P^i} P^i = (n-1) \frac{\partial \tau^j}{\partial P^i} \tau^j K^j + \frac{\partial \tau^j}{\partial P^j} \tau^j K^j = \tau^j.$$

Thus, by Euler's equation τ^j is homogeneous of degree one.

To evaluate the marginal rate of transformation, we have to compute $\partial K^j / \partial P^j$ and $\partial K^i / \partial P^j$, given by[34]

$$\frac{\partial K^j}{\partial P^j} = K_1^j \left(\frac{d\rho}{d\bar{\tau}} \cdot \frac{\partial \bar{\tau}}{\partial P^j} + \frac{\partial \tau^j}{\partial P^j} \right) + K_2^j,$$

$$\frac{\partial K^i}{\partial P^j} = K_1^i \left(\frac{d\rho}{d\bar{\tau}} \cdot \frac{\partial \bar{\tau}}{\partial P^j} + \frac{\partial \tau^i}{\partial P^j} \right) \qquad \forall i \neq j.$$

Using (2.27), (2.31), and (2.32), $\partial K^j / \partial P^j$ and $\partial K^i / \partial P^j$ reduce to

$$\frac{\partial K^j}{\partial P^j} = \frac{n-1}{n} \frac{K_1^j + K_2^j K^j}{K^j + \tau^j K_1^j},$$

$$\frac{\partial K^i}{\partial P^j} = -\frac{1}{n} \frac{K_1^i + K_2^i K^i}{K^i + \tau^i K_1^i} \qquad \forall i \neq j.$$

Substituting $\partial \tau^j / \partial P^j$, given by (2.31), into government j's first-order condition, (2.22), and using $K^j = \theta^j \bar{K}$, we get

$$1 - \tau^j \frac{\partial K^j}{\partial P^j} = 1 - \tau^j \frac{n-1}{n} \frac{K_1^j + K_2^j K^j}{K^j + \tau^j K_1^j} = F_p^j. \qquad (2.34)$$

The marginal provision cost of public services can be decomposed into two parts: the provision cost when governments have free access to head taxation, and the additional cost stemming from the fact that they have to rely on distortionary taxation; or, alternatively, the direct and the indirect provision cost of public services. While the first part represents the provision cost under efficiency, which is equal to unity, the second part incorporates the change of capital demand (flight or influx) as the local government varies its provision level. Hence, the second term stems from the 'feed-back effect' of industrial public services. According to (2.34), each government should fix P^j such that the efficient provision cost minus marginal revenue, resulting from the induced change of capital demand, equals the marginal product of public services in private production. To evaluate (2.34), (2.34), and (2.34), we use the following condition.

Condition 2.3 *Evaluated in some suitable neighbourhood of an equilibrium in public expenditures, capital demand satisfies*

$$-\varepsilon_{\rho + \tau^j}^j \frac{\tau^j}{\rho + \tau^j} < 1.$$

Using Condition (2.3) allows us to characterize a government's Laffer curve easily.

Lemma 2.5 *If the provision level of public services, P^j, and the net return to capital are held constant, public revenue increases in the local tax rate,*

$$K^j + \tau^j K_1^j > 0,$$

if, and only if, Condition 2.3 holds.

Proof: Follows from Condition 2.3. □

Loosely speaking, Condition 2.3, or equivalently Lemma 2.5, says that, holding prices and the provision level of public services constant, the government faces an increasing section of the (restricted) Laffer curve.

Condition 2.3 immediately yields the change of the net return to capital resulting from an unilateral change of the provision level of public goods in one region.

Lemma 2.6 *If a local government increases its provision level of public services, the nation-wide net return to capital falls if, and only if, Conditions 2.2 holds.*

Proof: Follows immediately from equation (2.33).   □

Taking also into account Condition 2.2, we see that the movement of capital, in response to a change in the provision of local public services, hinges on the elasticities of capital demand as follows.

Proposition 2.5 *If a local government increases its provision level of public services, local capital demand decreases if, and only if,*

- *either Conditions 2.2 and 2.3 hold,*

- *or Conditions 2.2 and 2.3 do not hold.*

If, however, either condition is fulfilled whilst the other is not, an increase of P^j induces an influx of capital. Note that under competition in public expenditures an influx (outflow) of capital causes the marginal product of capital in the other regions and therefore ρ to fall (rise): $\partial F_k^i / \partial P^j = F_{kk}^i \partial K^i / \partial P^j$.

Similarly, we get the response of the other governments in terms of their tax rates when government j alters its provision level of the local public good.

Lemma 2.7 *If the government of region j increases its provision level of public services, the other governments respond to this by decreasing their tax rates if, and only if,*

- *either Conditions 2.2 and 2.3 hold,*

- *or Conditions 2.2 and 2.3 do not hold.*

In sum, analogous to the case of competition in tax rates, four distinct cases may emerge, characterized by Conditions 2.2 and 2.3.

Case 1: Under Conditions 2.2 and 2.3, the elasticity of capital demand with respect to the provision level of public services is low: $\varepsilon^j_{Pj} < -\varepsilon^j_{\rho+\tau^j} \tau^j/(\rho+\tau^j) < 1$. A rise of the provision level of public services induces capital flight towards the other regions. Since, by assumption, these regions maintain their provision levels of public services, they decrease their tax rates correspondingly, thereby further aggravating capital flight from the tax-increasing region. This results in a decrease of the net return to capital.

Case 2: If Condition 2.2 is violated but 2.3 holds, the elasticity of capital demand with respect to p^j_k is sufficiently low: $-\varepsilon^j_{\rho+\tau^j} \tau^j/(\rho+\tau^j) <$ $\min\left\{1, \varepsilon^j_{Pj}\right\}$. In this case, a rise in P^j broadens the local tax basis substantially. Since lower capital demand in the other regions makes them respond by increasing their taxes rates, this further aggravates capital flight. Capital flight, on the other hand, raises F^i_k and, therefore, leads to a higher net return to capital.

Case 3: In this case, Condition 2.2 holds but 2.3 does not. Then, capital demand is highly elastic with respect to its price; namely, $-\varepsilon^j_{\rho+\tau^j} \tau^j/(\rho+$ $\tau^j) > \max\left\{1, \varepsilon^j_{Pj}\right\}$. Although ε^j_{Pj} is relatively low, a similar reaction to that in Case 2 is triggered, yet the reason for an influx of capital is slightly different. If government j increases its provision level by some small amount, it creates a slight influx of capital. However, even the slightest loss of capital makes the other governments raise their tax rates to compensate for the erosion of the tax basis. This strengthens the primary effect and, ultimately, results in a decrease of ρ.

Case 4: If both conditions do not hold, in which case we have $1 < -\varepsilon^j_{\rho+\tau^j} \tau^j/(\rho+\tau^j) < \varepsilon^j_{Pj}$, a higher level of public services drives out capital but causes ρ to rise.

By inspection of equation (2.34), we see that not only does the movement of capital depend on Conditions 2.2 and 2.3, but also the provision level of the public good; and quite obviously, we get a proposition that is very similar to the one derived for the case of tax competition (see Proposition 2.4).

Proposition 2.6 *Let local governments of identical regions (with $n \geq 2$)*

engage in competition in public expenditures. Public services are under-provided if, and only if,

- *either Conditions 2.2 and 2.3 hold*

- *or both of them do not hold.*

Thus, under Condition 2.3, underprovision of public services occurs if, and only if, Condition 2.2 holds; whereas public services are overprovided if, and only if, Condition 2.2 is violated. (And *vice versa* if Condition 2.3 is violated.) Again, there is a direct link between the provision level of public services and the elasticities of capital demand: when a higher provision level induces capital flight (Case 1 and 4), public services are underprovided; on the contrary, when this policy measure causes an influx of capital (Case 2 and 3), public services are provided inefficiently high. In the special case where $K_1^j + K_2^j K^j = 0$, local public goods are provided efficiently. Note that even a large number of competing regions $(n \to +\infty)$ is not sufficient for interjurisdictional competition to be efficient. The reason is that the left hand side of equation (2.34) does not converge to unity when n becomes large. (See also Proposition 2.7 on page 39.)

Relation to models with residential public goods

To illuminate the relation between the case of industrial public goods and the case where governments provide residential public goods, it is instructive to rewrite the marginal provision cost of public services as

$$\frac{1 + \frac{1}{n}\frac{\tau^j}{\rho + \tau^j}\varepsilon_{\rho+\tau^j}^j}{1 + \frac{\tau^j}{\rho + \tau^j}\varepsilon_{\rho+\tau^j}^j} - \frac{n-1}{n}\frac{1}{1 + \frac{\tau^j}{\rho + \tau^j}\varepsilon_{\rho+\tau^j}^j}\tau^j K_2^j \;=\; F_\rho^j. \;(2.35)$$

The marginal provision cost of the public good, the left hand side of (2.35), consists of two terms: the first term equals the equilibrium marginal rate of substitution between the private and the public good when local governments provide *residential* public goods and all capital is held by domestic consumers, i.e., $\theta^j = 1/n \; \forall j$. (Cf. equation (A.4) in Appendix A.) If, however, all capital is possessed by absent capital owners (foreigners), θ^j equals zero for all j, and each local government fixes its provision level of residential public goods where the marginal rate of substitution is equal to (cf. (A.6) in Appendix A),

$$\frac{n-1}{n} \frac{1}{1 + \dfrac{\tau^j}{\rho + \tau^j} \varepsilon^j_{\rho + \tau^j}}.$$

Denoting these terms by $\mathrm{MRS}^j_e|_{\theta^j=1/n}$ and $\mathrm{MRS}^j_e|_{\theta^j=0}$ respectively (where the subindex e stands for expenditure competition), a local government's optimality condition (2.35) can be rewritten as

$$1 - \tau^j \frac{\partial K^j}{\partial P^j} = \mathrm{MRS}^j_e|_{\theta^j=1/n} - \tau^j K^j_2 \mathrm{MRS}^j_e|_{\theta^j=0} = F^j_p.$$

$\mathrm{MRS}^j_e|_{\theta^j=1/n}$ represents the marginal cost of residential public goods in standard policy rules. The second part, however, $\tau^j K^j_2 \mathrm{MRS}^j_e|_{\theta^j=0}$, is related to the 'feed-back effect'. This term does not appear in models of residential public goods. As noted earlier, the 'feed-back effect' lowers the provision cost of industrial public services compared to those of residential public goods.

4.3 A Comparison of Both Types of Equilibria

We have seen that both types of interjurisdictional competition are strategically not equivalent. But when the equilibrium outcome under both regimes is not the same, the question arises: in which case is the provision level of public services higher? That is, under which form of interjurisdictional competition do strategic considerations make local governments fix their tax rates/provision levels the lowest? Wildasin (1988) has shown that, in the case of residential public goods, local governments behave 'more aggressively' under competition in public expenditures compared to competition in tax rates. However, we have seen that things change when governments provide public goods that benefit industries. Consequently, the question of which regime induces more competition between regions has to be reconsidered, and is the subject of this section.

We call expenditure competition *more competitive* than tax competition if the equilibrium policies imply that in each region the marginal rate of transformation under expenditure competition (e) is larger than under tax competition (t), and *vice versa*: $MRT^e > MRT^t \Leftrightarrow F^e_p > F^t_p$. Then, in the symmetric case, expenditure competition is more competitive than tax competition if, and only if,

$$\frac{K^j \left(1 - \tau^j K_2^j\right)}{K^j + \tau^j K_1^j - \frac{\tau^j}{n}\left(K_1^j + K_2^j K^j\right)} < \frac{K^j + \tau^j K_1^j - \tau^j \frac{n-1}{n}\left(K_1^j + K_2^j K^j\right)}{K^j + \tau^j K_1^j},$$

$$(2.36)$$

where the terms on the left hand side are evaluated at the tax equilibrium and the terms on the right hand side are evaluated at the equilibrium in public expenditures. Condition (2.36) requires comparing policy rules which are evaluated at different points. This is a delicate task, because the values of all variables change, in general, if we switch from one regime to the other.

Fortunately, since we focus on symmetric equilibria, the capital allocations of both regimes coincide, that is, in each region equilibrium capital demand equals $K^j = \bar{K}/n$, independent of the actual form of jurisdictional competition. Yet, the partial derivatives of capital demand with respect to the price of capital and the provision level of public services need not be identical under both regimes. In general, different provision levels of public services will cause K_1^j and K_2^j to vary. However, if the second partial derivative of F^j with respect to K^j does not depend on the provision level of public services, $K_1^j = 1/F_{kk}^j$ is independent of P^j and does not, therefore, hinge on the the actual mode of competition. This is, for example, fulfilled for $F^j(K^j, P^j) = \alpha_1 \log(1 + K^j) + \alpha_2 \log(1 + P^j) + \alpha_3 K^j P^j$ ($\alpha_i > 0$, $i = 1, 2, 3$). In addition, this production function incorporates another feature: the cross-derivative F_{kp}^j does not depend on P^j, such that $K_2^j = -F_{kp}^j/F_{kk}^j$ depends on K^j, but not on P^j. In this case, we can scrutinize condition (2.36) algebraically, at least to some extent.

For tractability, assume in the subsequent analysis that F_{kk}^j and F_{kp}^j do not depend on P^j, which may be a good approximation for all those cases where the marginal impact of P^j on the second partial derivatives of the production function, F_{kkp}^j and F_{kpp}^j, is zero.[35] This allows us to make a simplified comparison of both policy rules and to highlight our central findings, namely, that (i) competition in tax rates may be more competitive than competition in public expenditures, and that (ii) overprovision of public services may occur. To enrich the analysis, we also discuss three examples in the main text below (and provide further examples in Appendix B).

An approximative comparison

As indicated above, suppose that F_{kk}^j and F_{kp}^j do not depend on P^j. Moreover, let ξ be the percentage by which the tax rate under tax competition differs from the tax rate under expenditure competition: $\tau^{j,t} = \tau^{j,e}(1 + \xi) > 0$. Hence, if $\xi > 0$, expenditure competition is more competitive than tax competition (and *vice versa*). Conversely, $MRT^t > MRT^e$ if, and only if,

$$\frac{K^j\left(1 - \tau^j(1+\xi)K_2^j\right)}{K^j + \tau^j(1+\xi)K_1^j - \tau^j\frac{1+\xi}{n}\left(K_1^j + K_2^j K^j\right)} > \frac{K^j + \tau^j K_1^j - \tau^j\frac{n-1}{n}\left(K_1^j + K_2^j K^j\right)}{K^j + \tau^j K_1^j}$$

(2.37)

for $\xi < 0$.

To scrutinize the conditions under which tax competition is more competitive than expenditure competition, we may wish to investigate the terms in (2.37) successively. Denote by N_1 and D_1 the numerator and the denominator of the left- and by N_2 and D_2 the numerator and the denominator of the right hand side of (2.37). If both denominators exhibit the same sign, $D_1 D_2 > 0$, (2.37) is equivalent to

$$n^2\left(K^j - \tau^j(1+\xi)K_2^j K^j\right)\left(K^j + \tau^j K_1^j\right) > \left(nK^j + \tau^j K_1^j - (n-1)\tau^j K_2^j K^j\right)$$
$$\times\left(nK^j + (n-1)\tau^j(1+\xi)K_1^j - \tau^j(1+\xi)K_2^j K^j\right)$$

$$\Leftrightarrow \quad \tau^j(n-1)\left(K_1^j + K_2^j K^j\right)^2\left(\frac{\xi n K^j}{K_1^j + K^j K_2^j} + \tau^j(1+\xi)\right) < 0, \quad (2.38)$$

for $\xi < 0$; if both denominators exhibit different signs, $D_1 D_2 < 0$, (2.37) is equivalent to the reverse of (2.38).

In the following, we argue that competition in tax rates may well be more competitive than competition in public expenditures. The crucial terms are D_1 and D_2, ξ, and the last bracket term in equation (2.38). Since the left- as well as the right hand side of (2.37) must be positive, $D_i > 0$ requires $N_i > 0$ $(i = 1, 2)$ and *vice versa*. $N_1 > 0$, however, is equivalent to $1 - \tau^j(1 + \xi)K_2^j > 0$, implying that Condition 2.1 holds whenever D_1 is positive. On the other hand, $D_2 > 0$ is directly equivalent to $K^j + \tau^j K_1^j > 0$, i.e., Condition 2.3 is fulfilled whenever D_2 is positive.[36] We proceed by a case distinction.

Case (i): $D_1 > 0$ and $D_2 > 0$. In this case, suppose that D_1 and D_2 are both positive, implying that Conditions 2.1 and 2.3 are satisfied: $1 - \tau^j(1+\xi)K_2^j > 0$ and $K^j + \tau^j K_1^j > 0$. Then, $MRT^t > MRT^e$, that is, $\xi < 0$, if

$$\left(\frac{\xi n K^j}{K_1^j + K^j K_2^j} + \tau^j(1+\xi) \right) < 0. \tag{2.39}$$

Whether (2.39) is fulfilled depends crucially on Condition 2.2. Since ξ must be negative, the left hand side of (2.39) can only be negative if $K_1^j + K^j K_2^j > 0$, i.e., if Condition 2.2 does not hold. Inspecting Propositions 2.4 and 2.6, it becomes clear that when this occurs, public goods must be overprovided under both forms of interjurisdictional competition. If, on the other hand, $K_1^j + K^j K_2^j < 0$, condition (2.39) cannot be fulfilled. In this case, we get the classical result that competition in public expenditures is more competitive that competition in tax rates. Moreover, when Conditions 2.1–2.3 are satisfied, then, according to Propositions 2.4 and 2.6, it must be true that public goods are underprovided under both forms of interjurisdictional competition.

Case (ii): $D_1 < 0$ and $D_2 < 0$. When D_1 and D_2 are both negative, Conditions 2.1 and 2.3 are both violated: $1 - \tau^j(1 + \xi)K_2^j < 0$ and $K^j + \tau^j K_1^j < 0$. Also in this case, $MRT^t > MRT^e$ ($\xi < 0$) requires condition (2.39) to be met. Obviously, when $K_1^j + K^j K_2^j < 0$ (Condition 2.2), condition (2.39) can never be fulfilled. Only if Condition 2.2 does not hold, is there some scope for $MRT^t > MRT^e$. From Propositions 2.4 and 2.6 we know that, in this case, public services are underprovided under both competition regimes (and they are overprovided under both regimes if Condition 2.2 holds).

Case (iii): $D_1 < 0$ and $D_2 > 0$. When D_1 is negative but D_2 is positive, Condition 2.1 does not hold while Condition 2.3 is fulfilled. In this case, MRT^t can only exceed MRT^e ($\xi < 0$) if condition (2.39) is reversed. The easiest way to deal with this case is to apply Propositions 2.4 and 2.6. When Condition 2.2 also holds, we have overprovision under tax competition but underprovision under expenditure competition. Thus, we have the classical result that the latter is necessarily more competitive that the former. If, however, Condition 2.2 is violated, public goods are underprovided under tax competition but overprovided under expenditure competition. That is, when Conditions 2.1 and 2.1 do not hold but 2.3 is met, tax competition is more competitive than expenditure competition. (Yet, we shall see below that this case does not exist for an other reason.)

Case (iv): $D_1 > 0$ *and* $D_2 < 0$. In the last case, where D_1 is positive and D_2 is negative, Condition 2.1 is met while Condition 2.3 is not. Again, $MRT^t > MRT^e$ requires that the left hand side of (2.39) is positive. If, in addition, Condition 2.2 holds ($K_1^j + K^j K_2^j$ is negative), the reverse of (2.39) is indeed fulfilled for any $\xi < 0$ and tax competition is more competitive than expenditure competition. Alternatively, this can also be seen by inspection of Propositions 2.4 and 2.6: public services are underprovided under tax competition but overprovided under expenditure competition. If, on the other hand, Condition 2.2 is not fulfilled, tax competition cannot be more competitive than expenditure competition, which is again easily seen by application of Propositions 2.4 and 2.6.

Rather than focusing on Conditions 2.1–2.3, one can alternatively scrutinize the restrictions to which F_{kp}^j is subject in each of the cases discussed so far. To start with the most interesting of these, consider the case where $D_1 D_2 < 0$. Since, for instance, $D_1 > 0$ and $D_2 < 0$ also imply $N_1 > 0$ and $N_2 < 0$, respectively, we can, instead of investigating D_1 and D_2 directly, focus on $D_1 > 0$ and $N_2 < 0$. Recognizing that both terms impose a restriction on F_{kp}^j, we can solve both inequalities for the cross-derivative of the production function, yielding

$$\frac{1}{K^j}\left(1 - \frac{n\left(K^j + \tau^j K_1^j\right)}{\tau^j(n-1)K_1^j}\right) < F_{kp}^j < \frac{1}{K^j}\left(1 - \frac{n\left(K^j + \tau^j(1+\xi)K_1^j\right)}{\tau^j(1+\xi)K_1^j}\right).$$

$$(2.40)$$

Inequality (2.40) requires that F_{kp}^j lies in some medium range, that is, if capital demand is neither too inelastic nor too elastic with respect to the provision level of public services, $D_1 > 0$ and $D_2 < 0$ occurs. Yet, we should confirm whether this interval exists. For it to do so, the lower bound must be smaller than the upper bound, which is equivalent to

$$\frac{1}{n-1}(K^j + \tau^j K_1^j) < \frac{1}{1+\xi}(K^j + \tau^j(1+\xi)K_1^j). \qquad (2.41)$$

For $n > 1$ and $\xi < 0$, inequality (2.41) may be fulfilled and, hence, the case where tax competition is more competitive than expenditure competition is actually a possible outcome if F^j_{kp} satisfies (2.40). Note that this is consistent with our prior finding that $MRT^t > 1 > MRT^e$ emerges when Conditions 2.1 and 2.2 are fulfilled but Condition 2.3 is violated (Case (iv) on the page before).

The alternative case is where $D_1 < 0$ and $D_2 > 0$ (for $\xi < 0$). However, arguments similar to those of the preceeding analysis show that this case is not possible. To see this, consider again condition (2.41). Now, this inequality has to be reversed, and one can easily see that this can never be fulfilled for any $n > 1$ and $\xi < 0$. This confirms our result obtained in Case (iii) (see page 36) in so far as we now can rule out $MRT^t > MRT^e$ for $D_1 < 0$ and $D_2 > 0$, since $N_2 > 0$ imposes a restriction on F^j_{kp} which can never be fulfilled for any $\xi < 0$.

In Cases (i) and (ii), the analysis of the bounds of F^j_{kp} does not provided much insight. The only thing we can say is that when D_1 and N_2 are both positive, F^j_{kp} must be lower than the minimum of both limits given in (2.40); if, however, D_1 and N_2 are both negative, $MRT^t > MRT^e$ requires that F^j_{kp} must exceed the maximum of these limits.

Up to now we have not exploited condition (2.40) completely; it also allows us to draw some conclusions concerning the question whether public services will be under- or overprovided. When Condition 2.3 is not fulfilled ($D_2 < 0$) – the only interesting case here – $K^j + \tau^j K^j_1$ is negative, the bracket term on the left hand side of (2.40) falls short of unity. Recall that Condition 2.2 is equivalent to $K^j_1 + K^j_2 K^j < 0$ and $F^j_{kp} < 1/K^j$ and that, according to Proposition 2.6, public services are overprovided (underprovided) when Condition 2.2 is violated (fulfilled). Therefore, if F^j_{kp} falls between the left hand side of (2.40) and the minimum of $1/K^j$ and the right hand side of (2.40), public services are overprovided under expenditure competition, which is, in addition, more competitive than tax competition. Conversely, if F^j_{kp} exceeds $1/K^j$ but falls short of the right hand side of (2.40), public services are underprovided under expenditure competition, and tax competition is more competitive than expenditure competition. This confirms our result obtained in Case (iv) (on page 37).

In sum, we have shown that there is some evidence for the results that interjurisdictional competition may lead to overprovision of public goods and that tax competition may be more competitive than expenditure competition. We do not wish to scrutinize the conditions for this in more detail here; rather the analysis so far should suffice to show that the classical result may be reversed. To emphasize our findings, some examples will be provided below.

Let us conclude this section by revealing the condition under which the difference between competition in tax rates and competition in public expenditures disappears.

Proposition 2.7 *As n approaches infinity, the equilibrium allocations of competition in tax rates and in public expenditures coincide.*

Proof: First of all, recall that for $n \longrightarrow +\infty$, $\partial\rho/\partial\tau^j$ approaches zero. (See equation (2.27).) Using this fact, the social marginal provision cost under competition in tax rates, given by equation (2.28), tends to $K^j(1 - \tau^j K_2^j)/(K^j + \tau^j K_1^j)$. On the other hand, the marginal provision cost under competition in public expenditures is also equal to this term. $\square$

Even though both regimes of interjurisdictional competition differ, in general, for the large-number case, competition in tax rates and in public expenditures are strategically equivalent.

Three numerical comparisons

The above arguments may be sufficient to indicate under which conditions the classical results – competition in public expenditures is more competitive than competition in tax rates; public services are underprovided – may break down. Yet, to convince the reader fully, we proceed by calibrating three examples which serve to emphasize our results. (More examples can be found in Appendix B.) Our first example represents the standard case where competition in expenditures is more competitive than in tax rates and public goods are underprovided under both competition regimes. Then we show that, even if we consider Cobb–Douglas production functions, it may emerge that competition in tax rates turns out to be more competitive than competition in public expenditures. A third example demonstrates that interjurisdictional competition does not necessarily lead to underprovision of public services; if, for example, firms exhibit logistic production functions, local governments may well provide public services at inefficient high levels.

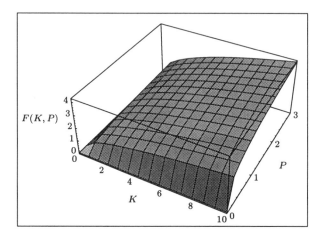

Figure 2.1: A CD production function

Example 1: The classical result. Let there be two regions, and assume that total capital supply equals $\bar{K} = 200$. Moreover, suppose, for the next two examples, that firms' technologies may be represented by a Cobb–Douglas (CD) production function[37]

$$F(K,P) = K^{\alpha_1}P^{\alpha_2}, \qquad 0 < \alpha_i < 1, i = 1, 2.$$

(See Figure 2.1.)

For our first example assume that the production function exhibits decreasing returns to scale: let $\alpha_1 = 0.5$ and $\alpha_2 = 0.25$. Using that, by symmetry, at any equilibrium each region's capital demand amounts to 100, we are able to compute the equilibrium policies under both competition regimes and the induced economic variables. Our results are summarized in Table 2.1; in addition, Figures 2.2 and 2.3 on the facing page depict both governments' reaction curves in the tax rates and in the expenditure plane, respectively.[38]

Comparing both competition regimes we see that the equilibrium in tax rates, denoted by E_t, implies higher tax rates and thus higher pro-

	τ	P	F_p	Q	Π	$\rho\theta\bar{K}$	$\mathcal{W}$
tax comp.	0.0231	2.3121	1.3333	12.33	6.1655	3.8535	10.0190
exp. comp.	0.0219	2.1864	1.3904	12.16	6.0800	3.8936	9.9736

Table 2.1: Results for a CD production function (Ex. 1)

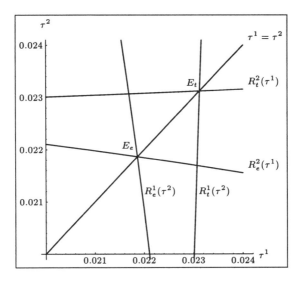

Figure 2.2: Reaction curves in the tax rates plane (Ex. 1)

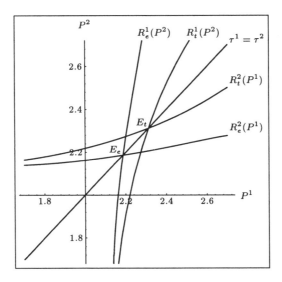

Figure 2.3: Reaction curves in the expenditure plane (Ex. 1)

vision levels than does the equilibrium in public expenditures, E_e. (In Figures 2.2 and 2.3, E_t lies in the upper right of E_e.) Correspondingly, under tax competition output, profit, and welfare are higher than under expenditure competition; yet, while a higher provision level requires a higher tax rate, the net return to capital and hence capital income are lower under tax competition $(\partial \rho / \partial \tau^j < 0$ if Condition 2.2 is fulfilled).[39] On the other hand, since a higher tax rate causes capital flight, interjurisdictional competition leads to underprovision of public services under both regimes ($F_p > 1$). In sum, this example suffices Case 1 under tax competition (see page 23) and under expenditure competition (see page 31). That is, it affirms the classical result that competition in public expenditures is more competitive than competition in tax rates and that, under both competition regimes, public services are underprovided.

Example 2: Tax competition is more competitive than expenditure competition. However, things change drastically if we increase the productivity parameters of the production function. To see this, consider a CD production function with $\alpha_1 = 0.7$ and $\alpha_2 = 0.4$.[40] Using this calibration leads to numerical results which are summarized in Table 2.2; in addition, Figures 2.4 and 2.5 on the facing page show the best-reply functions of both governments under each competition regime. Observe that in the neighbourhood of the equilibria, E_t in Figure 2.4 and E_e in Figure 2.5, the reaction curves are decreasing, i.e., tax rates and provision levels are no longer strategic complements but substitutes.

In this case, Conditions 2.1–2.3 do not hold, and we are faced with Case 4 (cf. pages 23 and 31), and with Case (ii) (page 36). A higher tax rate (provision level) induces capital flight and public services are again underprovided under both modes of competition. But now competition in tax rates turns out to be more competitive than competition in public expenditures. Consequently, the latter leads to a higher provision level of public services, higher output and profit, and a higher welfare level;

	τ	P	F_p	Q	Π	$\rho \theta \bar{K}$	$\mathcal{W}$
tax comp.	0.1667	16.6734	1.8571	77.41	23.2237	37.5152	60.7389
exp. comp.	0.1997	19.9688	1.6667	83.20	24.9610	38.2735	63.2345

Table 2.2: Results for a second CD production function (Ex. 2)

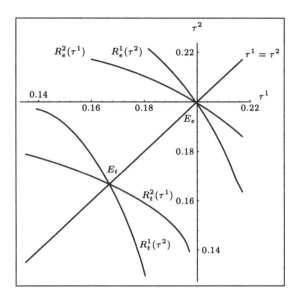

Figure 2.4: Reaction curves in the tax rates plane (Ex. 2)

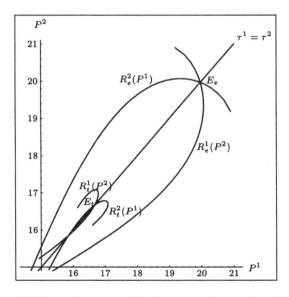

Figure 2.5: Reaction curves in the expenditure plane (Ex. 2)

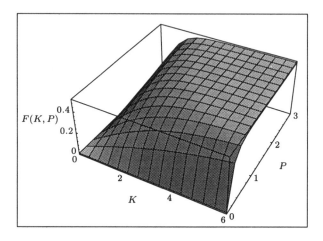

Figure 2.6: A logistic production function

and, contrary to the first example, capital owners benefit from a higher provision level (ρ increases).

Example 3: Overprovision of public services. To convince the reader that interjurisdictional competition may also lead to *overprovision* of public services, we present a last example. Suppose that local industries' production possibilities may be represented by a logistic production function

$$F(K,P) = \frac{1}{1 + \exp(-KP^\alpha)} - 0.5,$$

where $\alpha = 0.64$. (A logistic production function is depicted in Figure 2.6.)

Let total capital supply be equal to 4, implying that at any symmetric equilibrium capital demand amounts to 2 in each region. Using this, the equilibrium policies of the two governments and the induced allocations are given in Table 2.3.

Here, Condition 2.2 is fulfilled, but Conditions 2.1 and 2.3 are not. That is, we are faced with Case 3 (cf. pages 23 and 31), and with Case

	τ	P	F_p	Q	Π	$\rho\theta\bar{K}$	$\mathcal{W}$
tax comp.	0.0228	0.0455	0.9548	0.0688	0.0009	0.02239	0.02326
exp. comp.	0.0225	0.0449	0.9595	0.0682	0.0008	0.02243	0.02328

Table 2.3: Results for a logistic production function (Ex. 3)

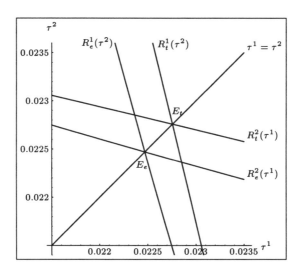

Figure 2.7: Reaction curves in the tax rates plane (Ex. 3)

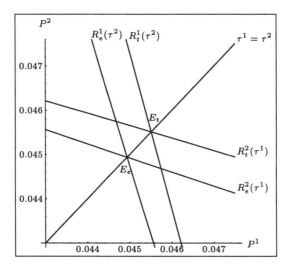

Figure 2.8: Reaction curves in the expenditure plane (Ex. 3)

(ii) (page 36): a higher tax rate (provision level) triggers capital flight and decreases the net return to capital. Therefore, capital owners are better off under tax competition. Moreover, interjurisdictional competition leads to *overprovision* of public services under both competition regimes; and, again, expenditure competition turns out to be more competitive than tax competition. (See also Figures 2.7 and 2.8 on the page before.) However, this does not imply that tax competition leads to a higher welfare level than does expenditure competition: although stockholders receive higher dividends in the case of tax competition, expenditure competition leads to a higher welfare level, for the extent of overprovision is less in the latter case.

5   CONCLUDING REMARKS

We have considered a model of interjurisdictional competition where local governments provide local public goods that benefit industry. The required public expenditures are financed through distortionary taxation of mobile industrial capital. We have investigated two competition regimes: local governments fix either tax rates or expenditure levels. Since both regimes are strategically not equivalent, the corresponding taxation formulae differ and two distinct equilibrium allocations occur. (Only in the limiting case where regions are identical and their number tends to infinity, are both competition regimes strategically equivalent.)

A similar model was scrutinized by Wildasin (1988) where governments provide residential public goods. He found that, in the case of identical regions, interjurisdictional competition in public expenditures is 'more competitive' than in tax rates. We show the analogy does not necessarily hold if governments provide local public goods that benefit industry. This non-equivalence is due to the fact that industrial services affect production possibilities. When production is improved, capital flight is typically mitigated through the provision of public goods. Hence, the provision of industrial public goods causes a second-order effect on the public revenue, lowering the marginal social cost of public services. We call this the 'feed-back effect' of public goods. If this 'feed-back effect' is sufficiently strong, raising the tax rate on capital and thereby expanding the provision level of industrial public goods induces an influx of capital.

This does never appear if we deal with residential public goods.

Our main results are derived for the special case of identical regions: in the regular case, interjurisdictional competition in public expenditures is 'more competitive' than competition in tax rates and public goods are underprovided under both competition regimes. In some polar cases, however, either of the two results may be reversed: interjurisdictional competition in tax rates may be 'more competitive' than competition in public expenditures, and overprovision of public goods may occur. Moreover, we show that under both competition regimes, there is a direct link between capital flight and the provision level of public goods: local public goods are underprovided (overprovided) if, and only if, a higher level of the respective strategic variable, that is, of the tax rate or of the provision level, induces an outflow (influx) of capital.

APPENDICES

Appendix A: The Case of Residential Public Goods

In this appendix we contrast the case of industrial public goods, investigated so far, with the case where governments provide residential public goods, as considered by Wildasin (1988), Hoyt (1991b), and others. In particular, we wish to compare our formulae, equations (2.16) and (2.22), with their counterparts in the case of residential public goods.

When consumers benefit from the provision of public goods, utility depends on X^j and on P^j: $U^j(X^j, P^j)$; whereas, on the other hand, production exclusively hinges on the use of capital: $F^j(K^j)$. In this case, capital demand only depends on the gross price of capital, $K^j(\rho + \tau^j)$. The rest of the model remains unchanged.

Executing the same computations as in Section 3 gives us a government's optimal policy under *tax competition* as

$$MRS^{j,t}|_{\theta^j=1/n} = -\frac{dX^j}{dP^j} = \frac{K^j + \left(K^j - \theta^j \bar{K}\right)\frac{\partial \rho}{\partial \tau^j}}{K^j + \left(1 + \frac{\partial \rho}{\partial \tau^j}\right)\tau^j K^{j\prime}}, \qquad (A.1)$$

and similarly under *expenditure competition*,

$$MRS^{j,e}|_{\theta^j=1/n} = -\frac{dX^j}{dP^j} = \sum_{i=1}^{n}\left(\frac{F^{j\prime}}{\varepsilon^j}\frac{dK^j}{d\tau^i} - \theta^j \bar{K}\frac{\partial \rho}{\partial \tau^i}\right)\frac{\partial \tau^i}{\partial P^j}, \qquad (A.2)$$

where $\varepsilon^j := (\rho + \tau^j)K^{j\prime}/K^j$ denotes the elasticity of capital demand with respect to the (after-tax) price of capital. Again, tax competition and expenditure competition are strategically not equivalent. Moreover, formulae (A.1) and (A.2) significantly differ from their respective counterparts, (2.16) and (2.22). To work out the differences most clearly, consider the case of identical regions, where $\theta^j = 1/n$ for all j. In this case, (A.1) and (A.2) reduce to[41]

$$MRS^{j,t}|_{\theta^j=1/n} = \frac{1}{1 + \varepsilon^j\dfrac{n-1}{n}\dfrac{\tau^j}{\rho+\tau^j}} > 1. \qquad (A.3)$$

and

$$MRS^{j,e}|_{\theta^j=1/n} = K^j\frac{d\tau^j}{dP^j} = \frac{1 + \varepsilon^j\dfrac{1}{n}\dfrac{\tau^j}{\rho+\tau^j}}{1 + \varepsilon^j\dfrac{\tau^j}{\rho+\tau^j}} > 1 \qquad (A.4)$$

respectively, where we have used $\partial\rho/\partial\tau^j = -1/n$. These formulae could easily be contrasted with equations (2.28) and (2.34). (See discussion on page 14f.)

Since any increase in the level of public services unambiguously drives out capital when public goods benefit consumers, (A.3) and (A.4) show that for any positive tax rate the marginal rate of substitution exceeds unity, implying that public services are underprovided in any equilibrium. Again, efficiency could only be reached if (i) the number of competing jurisdictions tends to infinity, or (ii) capital is demanded inelastically ($\varepsilon^j = 0$), or (iii) there is only one single region (no competition).

For the case of identical regions where all capital is owned by foreigners ($\theta^j = 0\,\forall j$), Wildasin (1988) derives similar formulae, which are, for the sake of completeness, only briefly stated here:

$$MRS^{j,t}|_{\theta^j=0} = \frac{n-1}{n} \frac{1}{1 + \varepsilon^j \dfrac{n-1}{n} \dfrac{\tau^j}{\rho + \tau^j}}, \qquad (A.5)$$

$$MRS^{j,e}|_{\theta^j=0} = \frac{n-1}{n} \frac{1}{1 + \varepsilon^j \dfrac{\tau^j}{\rho + \tau^j}}. \qquad (A.6)$$

In this case, residents neither benefit nor suffer from a change of the net return to capital through their interest income, which alters the optimality rules correspondingly.

One can easily see that, *ceteris paribus*, the marginal rates of substitution between the private and the public good are lower when capital owners are absent:

$$MRS^{j,t}|_{\theta^j=0} < MRS^{j,t}|_{\theta^j=1/n} \quad \text{and} \quad MRS^{j,e}|_{\theta^j=0} < MRS^{j,e}|_{\theta^j=1/n}.$$

That is, for $\theta^j = 0$ provision levels are higher, implying that interjurisdictional competition is less competitive under both regimes when capital owners reside elsewhere.[42] The reason is that countries are in fact capital importers, which leads governments to neglect their impact on the net return to capital. If capital owners are present, each government hesitates to tax capital more severely since this depresses capital owners' income. However, when capital owners live in foreign countries, this incentive disappears and governments impose higher tax rates on capital, leading to higher provision levels of public services.

Appendix B: More Examples

This appendix provides some more examples. Suppose that the number of regions is $n = 10$ and that total capital supply is $\bar{K} = 1000$. By symmetry, we know that equilibrium capital demand must be 100 in each region.

Again, consider a Cobb–Douglas production function (omitting super-indices):

$$F(K, P) = \alpha_0 K^{\alpha_1} P^{\alpha_2},$$

with $\alpha_0 = 10$. For a given supply of the public good, P, a firm's factor demand is

$$K = \left(\frac{\alpha_0 \alpha_1}{\rho + \tau} P^{\alpha_2} \right)^{1/(1-\alpha_1)} \quad (= 100),$$

and its first partial derivatives are given by

$$K_1 = \frac{1}{F_{kk}} = \frac{1}{\alpha_1 - 1} \frac{1}{\rho + \tau} K = \frac{\alpha_1}{\alpha_1 - 1} \frac{F(K, P)}{(\rho + \tau)^2}, \quad \text{(B.1)}$$

$$K_2 = -\frac{F_{kp}}{F_{kk}} = -\frac{\alpha_2}{(\alpha_1 - 1)\tau}, \quad \text{(B.2)}$$

where we have used the governmental budget constraint, $P = \tau K$. Using these results, we can calculate the crucial terms

$$t_1 := 1 - \tau K_2 \quad \text{(B.3)}$$
$$t_2 := K_1 + K K_2 \quad \text{(B.4)}$$
$$t_3 := K + \tau K_1 \quad \text{(B.5)}$$

which correspond to our Conditions 2.1, 2.2, and 2.3, respectively.

Now, let us investigate several specifications of the production function.

Example A

Let $\alpha_1 = 0.5$ and $\alpha_2 = 0.25$. Using (B.1), (B.2), and $K = 100$, we have

F_k	$=$	$1.5811\tau^{0.25}$		
F_{kk}	$=$	$-0.0079\tau^{0.25}$		
F_{kp}	$=$	$0.0040\tau^{-0.75}$		
K_1	$=$	$-316.228\tau^{0.25}(\rho + \tau)^{-2}$		

$$F_p = 0.7906\tau^{-0.75}$$
$$F_{pp} = -0.0059\tau^{-1.75}$$
$$K_2 = 0.5\tau^{-1}$$

Inserting these results, the crucial terms, t_1, t_2, and t_3, are

$$t_1 = 0.5 \tag{B.6}$$

$$t_2 = 50\tau^{-1} - 126.491\tau^{-0.25} \approx -41 \tag{B.7}$$

$$t_3 = 100 - 126.491\tau^{0.75} \approx 31. \tag{B.8}$$

This enables us to compute the equilibrium tax rates and expenditure levels under both competition regimes:

Tax competition: $\tau^t = 0.4359$ and $P = 43.59$.

Expenditure competition: $\tau^e = 0.4324$ and $P = 43.24$.

This is the classical result, where competition in public expenditures is more competitive than competition in tax rates. Substituting the tax rates into t_2 and t_3, we see, as expected from our previous analysis, that Conditions 2.1, 2.2, and 2.3 are fulfilled.

Example B

Let $\alpha_1 = 0.5$ and $\alpha_2 = 0.1$. In this case, we have

$$F_k = 0.7924\tau^{0.1} \qquad F_p = 0.1585\tau^{-0.9}$$
$$F_{kk} = -0.0040\tau^{0.1} \qquad F_{pp} = -0.0014\tau^{-1.9}$$
$$F_{kp} = 0.0008\tau^{-0.9}$$
$$K_1 = -158.489\tau^{0.1}(\rho + \tau)^{-2} \qquad K_2 = 0.2\tau^{-1}$$

and

$$t_1 = 0.8 \tag{B.9}$$

$$t_2 = 20\tau^{-1} - 252.383\tau^{-0.1} \approx -129 \tag{B.10}$$

$$t_3 = 100 - 252.383\tau^{0.9} \approx 66. \tag{B.11}$$

Then, the equilibrium policies under both competition regimes are given by

Tax competition: $\tau^t = 0.1071$ and $P = 10.71$.

Expenditure competition: $\tau^e = 0.1068$ and $P = 10.68$.

Again, this is the classical result and Conditions 2.1, 2.2, and 2.3 are fulfilled as expected.

Example C

If, however, we parameterize the production with $\alpha_1 = 0.7$ and $\alpha_2 = 0.5$, results change. Using this specification of the production function, we have

$$
\begin{aligned}
F_k &= 17.5832\tau^{0.5} & F_p &= 12.5594\tau^{-0.5} \\
F_{kk} &= -0.0527\tau^{0.5} & F_{pp} &= -0.0628\tau^{-1.5} \\
F_{kp} &= 0.0879\tau^{-0.5} & & \\
K_1 &= -5861.07\tau^{0.5}(\rho + \tau)^{-2} & K_2 &= 1.6667\tau^{-1}
\end{aligned}
$$

and

$$
\begin{aligned}
t_1 &= -0.6667 & \text{(B.12)} \\
t_2 &= 166.667\tau^{-1} - 18.9575\tau^{-0.5} \approx 0.6 & \text{(B.13)} \\
t_3 &= 100 - 18.9575\tau^{0.5} \approx -35. & \text{(B.14)}
\end{aligned}
$$

Using these results, the equilibrium policies are as follows:

Tax competition: $\tau^t = 50.2681$ and $P = 5026.81$.

Expenditure competition: $\tau^e = 51.8341$ and $P = 5183.41$.

In this case, the result is reversed. Competition in public expenditures, leading to a higher provision level of public services, is less competitive than competition in tax rates. It is easily checked that, for both tax rates, we have $t_1 < 0$, $t_2 > 0$, and $t_3 < 0$. That is, none of Conditions 2.1–2.3 is fulfilled. This corresponds to Case 4 under both competition regimes (cf. pages 24 and 31).

Example D

The analogy holds if we set $\alpha_1 = 0.7$ and $\alpha_2 = 0.4$.

$$
\begin{aligned}
F_k &= 11.0943\tau^{0.4} & F_p &= 6.3396\tau^{-0.6} \\
F_{kk} &= -0.0333\tau^{0.4} & F_{pp} &= -0.0380\tau^{-1.6} \\
F_{kp} &= 0.0444\tau^{-0.6} & & \\
K_1 &= -3698.03\tau^{0.4}(\rho + \tau)^{-2} & K_2 &= 1.3333\tau^{-1}.
\end{aligned}
$$

Using these results, we have

$$
\begin{aligned}
t_1 &= -0.3333 & \text{(B.15)} \\
t_2 &= 133.33\tau^{-1} - 30.0456\tau^{-0.4} \approx 1.4 & \text{(B.16)} \\
t_3 &= 100 - 30.0456\tau^{0.6} \approx -19.6, & \text{(B.17)}
\end{aligned}
$$

and the equilibrium policy variables are

Tax competition: $\tau^t = 9.9898$ and $P = 998.98$.

Expenditure competition: $\tau^e = 10.0830$ and $P = 1008.30$.

Again, competition in tax rates turns out to be more competitive than competition in public expenditures, and $t_1 < 0$, $t_2 > 0$, and $t_3 < 0$ imply that none of Conditions 2.1–2.3 is fulfilled (Case 4 under both regimes).

NOTES

1. The major branch of the literature deals with the large-number case where regions engage in *perfect* competition. See, for example, Wilson (1985), (1986), Zodrow and Mieszkowski (1986), and Oates and Schwab (1988).
2. Under tax competition a marginal increase of one region's tax rate (and the resulting change of the provision level of local public services) does not induce other governments to alter their tax rates but to adjust their provision levels of public services suitably. However, if regions engage in competition in public expenditures, a marginal change of one region's provision level (and the resulting change of the tax rate) makes other governments reduce their taxes rates – provided that they are faced with an influx of capital – such that total revenues are kept constant. In this sense, a Nash equilibrium in public expenditures can be viewed as an equilibrium in tax rates with negative conjectural variations. Or, alternatively, a Nash equilibrium in tax rates corresponds to an equilibrium in public expenditures with *positive* conjectural variations.
3. We call those public goods that benefit industry *industrial public goods*. This category encompasses a large part of that public expenditure which is commonly summarized as *infrastructure*: transportation facilities, communication systems, research facilities, water and sewer provision, public safety, administration, foreign relations etc. However, both notions do not coincide, since infrastructure also includes public services that benefit, at least partially, residents.
4. '[...] figures indicate that, if infrastructure investment is a problem, it may be much more a state and local problem than a federal problem' (Gramlich, 1994, p. 1178).
5. Under this we subsume general public services, public order and safety, vocational schools, economic affairs and services, transport and communication, community amenities and development. Clearly, some of these

services also benefit residents; likewise, there are primarily residential public goods which are also advantageous to industry: schools, universities, social administration, housing etc. In any case, an unambiguous categorization of real public services in residential and industrial public goods does not seem possible; nor is it our topic here.

6. Source: Statistisches Bundesamt (1995); for further international data see International Monetary Fund (1994).

7. The interpretation of this model in the context of an international setting is straightforward.

8. Note that while firms behave perfectly competitively, this is an innocuous assumption.

9. Subindices of functions denote partial derivatives, while subindices of prices denote the items they are attached to.

10. The immobility of the population is a crucial assumption, since results may change drastically if residents begin to migrate in response to local governments' policies. See, for example, Hoyt (1991a) and Burbidge and Myers (1994). Richter and Wellisch (1993) consider mobile and immobile workers simultaneously.

11. This is an innocuous assumption, since our model can easily be reformulated on a per capita basis – similar to Bucovetsky (1991), who considers two regions differing only in size (number of identical residents) – without affecting results.

12. Alternatively, we may assume that the production process uses some locationally fixed input, e.g., labour or land, which is owned exclusively by local residents.

13. Alternatively, we may interpret public expenditure as a measure (or proxy variable) for the provision of public goods. (This avoids any evaluation and aggregation problem.)

14. If we assume that a locationally fixed input, which is owned exclusively by local residents, such as labour or land, is used in production (see also note 12), the term $F^j(K^j, P^j) - K^j F_k^j(K^j, P^j)$ equals the income of the fixed factor.

15. From now on, we denote by ρ and $K^1, \ldots, K^n$ the *equilibrium* values, implicitly given by firms' first-order conditions and the market-clearing condition for capital. Keeping this in mind, we do not refer to ρ and $K^1, \ldots, K^n$ as equilibrium values explicitly in the ensuing analysis, though we always consider these variables along the equilibrium path of the capital market. By using this convention, we unambiguously attach the word 'equilibrium' to the outcome of interjurisdictional competition and the related variables, where not stated otherwise.

16. Throughout this work we assume that, whenever necessary, any equilibrium variable meets the conditions of the implicit function theorem, which is applied several times.

17. The analysis is restricted to *pure* strategies.

18. Unfortunately, we are unable to prove the existence and uniqueness of an equilibrium, in general. Therefore, all statements regarding any equilibrium are of the kind '*Provided that an equilibrium exists, the following is true* ...'. In a two-regions commodity taxation model Mintz and Tulkens (1986) discussed in depth the conditions for the existence of a Nash equilibrium; while in a more specific model Bucovetsky (1991) succeeds in proving the existence of an equilibrium.

19. Equivalently, we may assume that, in addition to capital taxation, the local government is authorized to use head taxes (or lump sum transfers) on any desired level to raise (or reimburse) public funds.

20. To keep mathematical expressions readable, we omit any tags to indicate 'optimal' values of variables throughout this work. Therefore, it is pointed out to the reader that the same symbol may have diverse values if the variable is evaluated at different points.

21. We follow the classical distinction, first introduced by Viner (1931), between *technological* and *pecuniary (or fiscal)* externalities; where the first type generates a shift of technological relations (e.g., production or utility functions), the second, a group of pseudo-externalities, affects some individual's financial status.

22. If several tax rates are available, a local government may possibly immunize the region against fiscal externalities. In the model of Bucovetsky and Wilson (1991) the presence of a residence- and a source-based tax on capital income enables a government to affect the local gross and net return to capital independent of the nation-wide (or world) return.

23. For a more deliberate discussion of Wildasin's result see Appendix A.

24. Since Lemma 2.1 gives us a unique relation between the partial derivatives of capital demand and the second-order derivatives of the production function, we can also express all results in terms of the characteristics of the production technology.

25. Apparently, this is a somehow uncomfortable 'joint condition' that is not clearly fulfilled or violated *ex ante*, for it depends on the equilibrium outcome. However, this condition, as well as two others in the subsequent analysis, are not as questionable as they might appear: they do not represent assumptions but serve as benchmarks for case distinction. To give the reader some idea under which circumstances our conditions are fulfilled, three examples are presented in Section 4.3.

26. See, for example, Hoyt (1991b) who finds that, for the case of identical regions, $\partial \rho / \partial \tau^j = -1/n$ (equation (5) therein).

27. One exception is the model of Wilson (1986). He shows that in a polar case, the net return to capital may increase if the supply of public goods is raised; in his notation, $d\rho/dX_E > 0$ may occur. One other exception is the two-jurisdictions, two-periods debt model of Jensen and Toma (1991) where overprovision may occur in either one of the two regions.

28. Zodrow and Mieszkowski (1986) ignore the possibility of attracting capital through higher provision levels of industrial public goods by assuming that $1 - K^j F_{kp}^j$ and $-(F_{kk}^j + \tau^j F_{kp}^j)$ are always positive (equations (16) and (17) therein). However, this is an unnecessary restriction, since for the existence of an equilibrium of identical regions we only require that any government faces an increasing section of its Laffer curve, $\partial P^j / \partial \tau^j > 0$. To convince the reader of the relevance of equilibria where at least one of our conditions is violated, two examples are given in Section 4.3.

29. Note also that, under both competition regimes, the equilibrium allocations differ significantly from the corresponding equilibria where governments provide residential local public goods. (Compare (8.1) and (8.2) of Wildasin (1988) with equations (2.16) and (2.22), respectively.)

30. Independent of which competition regime we investigate – interjurisdictional tax competition in tax rates or in public expenditures – we focus on symmetric equilibria, although others may exist.

31. Independent of whether Conditions 2.1 and 2.2 are fulfilled, a necessary condition for the existence of an equilibrium is that each local government faces an increasing section of its Laffer curve, $\partial P^j / \partial \tau^j > 0$. This can be easily seen from equation (2.13) by using $K^j = \theta^j \bar{K}$. Alternatively, observe that the left hand side of (2.28) equals $K^j (\partial P^j / \partial \tau^j)^{-1}$, which must be positive – otherwise an equilibrium cannot exist. (See also note 28.)

32. Also from an empirical point of view, overprovision (or even efficient provision) of industrial public services cannot be ruled out, which is emphasized by Gramlich (1994) in a review article, p. 1193: 'As for the alleged infrastructure shortage, the evidence reviewed in the paper is decidedly mixed.'

33. Note that even if the number of regions becomes very large, interjurisdictional competition does not lead to efficiency. If n tends to infinity, implying that $\partial \rho / \partial \tau^j$ approaches zero, the term $(n - 1)\partial \rho / \partial \tau^j$ does not vanish, as long as $K_1^j + K_2^j K^j \neq 0$.

34. Note that here the terms $\partial K^j / \partial P^j$ and $\partial K^i / \partial P^j$ mean the total effect of P^j on K^j and K^i respectively. Thus, here $\partial K^j / \partial P^j$ is different from

K_2^j, since the former also includes the induced effect of P^j on p_k^j.

35. Alternatively, one could also assume that F_{kkp}^j and F_{kpp}^j are sufficiently close to zero and the tax rates under both regimes do not differ 'too much'.

36. Recall that Condition 2.1 and Condition 2.3 are stated within the context of tax competition and expenditure competition, respectively. That is, a statement such as 'Condition 2.1 holds' means that $1 - \tau^j K_2^j$ is, evaluated at the *equilibrium in tax rates*, positive: $1 - \tau^{t,j} K_2^j = 1 - \tau^j (1 + \xi) K_2^j > 0$. An ambiguity might arise in the case of Condition 2.2, for it is used under both competition regimes. Yet, under the assumptions made, K_1^j and K_2^j do not vary with τ^j (and P^j), implying that the term $K_1^j + K_2^j K^j$ does not depend on the specific mode of competition.

37. It is the classical approach of the empirical literature to estimate the coefficients of a CD production function which includes the public capital stock. See, for example, Aschauer (1989), Gramlich (1994), Baltagi and Pinnoi (1995), and the references therein.

38. Note that we are slightly inaccurate in calling $R_e^j(\tau^i)$ in Figure 2.2 (and $R_t^j(\tau^i)$ in Figure 2.3) *reaction curves*; these curves only represent those tax rates (respectively provision levels) which are induced by the best-reply expenditure levels (respectively tax rates) under expenditure (respectively tax) competition.

39. Inserting the results of Table 2.1 into $1 - \tau K_2$, $K_1 + K_2 K$, and $K + \tau K_1$ shows that Conditions 2.1, 2.2, and 2.3 are fulfilled under both competition regimes.

40. Note that we have not ruled out increasing returns to scale. The only requirements we imposed upon the production function were that F^j is increasing and concave with respect to capital, increasing in the public good, and exhibiting a positive cross-derivative.

41. See also Hoyt (1991b).

42. This is true if, and only if, any government faces an increasing section of its Laffer curve.

3. Strategic Environmental Policy

1 INTRODUCTION

With recent agreements to reduce trade barriers (e.g., the European Single Market, NAFTA, GATT), indirect trade policy became the focus of attention; in this context, a canonical policy tool seems to be environmental policy. At least since the 1992 UN Conference on Environment and Development, governments may have been tempted to (ab)use environmental policy in order to pursue trade political aims, namely to improve a country's trade balance. In particular, under the conditions of imperfect competition on the goods market, an environmental policy that promotes exports (lax environmental standards for the exporting industry) but hampers foreign imports (severe environmental standards for imports) may have significant ecological and economic benefits. Thus, with the abolishment of tariffs (and other direct trade barriers), a close link arises between, on the one hand, environmental policy and, on the other, trade and industrial policy. Moreover, with increasing public budget deficits, it becomes tempting to raise additional public funds through 'green' taxes. While the establishment of eco-taxes yields a significant tax revenue, environmental policy also has a growing impact on fiscal policy and therefore on the provision level of public services. In sum, emission taxation in an open economy, where direct trade policy is not feasible, depends crucially on the mode of competition, the possible revenue from emission taxation, the desired provision level of public services, and, of course, on the flow of pollutants and the social damage they cause.

Since several policy fields are involved, the theoretical literature dealing with strategic emission taxation in open economies draws upon different economic branches. The *regulation literature* scrutinizes firms' behaviour under different market structures when emission taxes (or standards) are introduced. Attention focuses on the firms' equilibrium emissions and output decisions, their aggregate values, and the number of competing firms. (See Ebert, 1992, Requate, 1994, and others.) One common characteristic of these (partial) models is that *one* regulator determines a uniform tax rate for *all* firms. But often firms do not reside in *one* jurisdiction and thus are not liable to the same tax regime. In particular, if, as in the EU or in the US, state governments (or even the authorities of the counties) fix emission taxes, different firms are confronted with different prices of environmental inputs.

This fact is acknowledged by the *new trade theory* – as far as it deals with emission taxation. Yet, this literature, building upon the work of Dixit (1984), Brander and Spencer (1985), and Eaton and Grossman (1986), exhibits other drawbacks: either firms (exclusively) compete on a third country's market (e.g., Ulph, 1992, Conrad, 1993, and Barrett, 1994) and/or the tax revenue is redistributed to residents by lump sum transfers. In the first case, local residents do not consume firms' output at all; in the second case, private marginal utility of income equals marginal value of public funds.[1]

These shortcomings are avoided by the *regional economics literature* which, originating from the influential papers of Zodrow and Mieszkowski (1986) and Wildasin (1988), focuses on the provision of public goods under distortionary taxation. Though some authors introduce environmental problems into this framework (e.g., Oates and Schwab, 1988), this branch centres on capital and income taxation, not on environmental taxation nor on imperfect competition.

The recently emerging, so-called *double dividend literature* deals with environmental problems under distortionary taxation (Bovenberg and de Mooij, 1994a,b and others). However, most of these models deal with perfect competition, and only some of them include endogenous provision of public goods (van der Ploeg and Bovenberg, 1993a,b and Bovenberg and van der Ploeg, 1994).

Since political decisions have to be made in a world of non-competitive markets, severe public financial needs, great environmental problems, and international competition, we try to avoid the above-mentioned limitations of the literature and present a more general model of interjurisdictional tax competition. To do this, we allow for different firms[2] producing a consumer good by, among other things, the use of environmental inputs (pollutant emissions).[3] Each firm exhibits Cournot behaviour and is regulated by a local government through the imposition of an emission tax. Local governments, in determining their tax rates, engage in interjurisdictional tax competition where the resulting public revenues are spent on the provision of local public goods. Hence, we consider endogenous provision of local public goods. This link between environmental quality and the provision of public goods may invalidate the results of simpler models. For example, the conclusions of Krutilla (1991), Kennedy (1994), and Pethig (1994), who assume efficient provision of public goods, need not be true any longer. More precisely, whether a government determines its emission tax below or above marginal damage of pollution, not only depends on a region's trade position and on the competitiveness of the output market, but also on the provision level of public goods. We find that if there is no pollutant transmission, a government fixes its emission tax above (beneath) marginal environmental damage if public funds are relatively scarce (not too scarce). More precisely, if the social damage curve is sufficiently steep, public services are overprovided whereas the environmental quality is too low. In the polar case where pollution is purely local and firms behave perfectly competitively, governments of identical regions fix their tax rates above (beneath) marginal damage if public goods are underprovided (overprovided).

Investigating the incentives that make local governments deviate from cooperative behaviour (second-best policy), we show that due to three main causes the equilibrium tax rates differ from those tax rates that maximize overall welfare: *environmental and fiscal externalities and interregional production shifting.* While at least one of them is effective, the equilibrium allocation is not even second-best. In some cases the weighted sum of these effects is positive, and a government tends to deviate from the characterized cooperative solution by increasing its tax rate. However, the opposite seems to be more 'likely' and then equilibrium tax rates are fixed rather too low than too high.

This chapter is organized as follows. Section 2 sets up the model and depicts the behaviour of the private sector – firms and consumers. In Section 3 we derive the equilibrium tax rates and the cooperative tax rates. A comparison of both reveals the sources of inefficiency, i.e., the incentives that prompt local governments to deviate from cooperative behaviour. Section 4 summarizes.

2 THE MODEL

2.1 Local Firms

Consider a nation (or union) that consists of n regions (or states) where in each jurisdiction there is one resident firm. These n local firms producing one homogeneous output good compete on a national market.[4] Each firm $j = 1, \ldots, n$ produces its output, Q^j, by, among others, the use of environmental inputs (pollutant emissions), E^j. Assume that the employment of all factors, except pollutant emissions, is fixed, implying that the variable production costs depend only on output and emissions, $C^j(Q^j, E^j)$. The cost function, C^j, is supposed to be strictly convex with $C_q^j > 0$ and $C_{qe}^j < 0$.[5] If the government of region j imposes a constant tax rate, τ^j, per unit of pollutant emissions, the local firm incurs additional cost of $\tau^j E^j$.

Each firm's revenue is determined by its supply and the market price which depends on total supply, $Q := \sum_{j=1}^n Q^j$. We assume that firms engage in Cournot competition, facing a downward sloping inverse demand curve, P, which is 'not too convex' in the sense that[6]

$$P''(Q) \leq -\frac{P'(Q)}{Q} \quad \forall Q \in \mathbb{R}_+. \tag{3.1}$$

Define $Q^{-j} := \sum_{i \neq j} Q^i$. Among other things, condition (3.1) ensures that revenue $R^j(Q^j, Q^{-j}) := P(Q)Q^j$ is a concave function of Q^j which, together with the convexity of C^j, implies that profit is concave in Q^j and E^j.[7] Compounding revenue and cost terms, we can write the profit of firm j – the firm which is located in jurisdiction j – as

$$\Pi^j(Q^j, E^j; Q^{-j}, \tau^j) = P(Q)Q^j - C^j(Q^j, E^j) - \tau^j E^j. \tag{3.2}$$

For each firm $j = 1, \ldots, n$ its profit-maximizing policy, with respect to Q^j and E^j, is determined by the first-order conditions (f.o.c.s)

$$P(Q) + P'(Q)Q^j - C_q^j(Q^j, E^j) = 0, \tag{3.3}$$

$$-\tau^j - C_e^j(Q^j, E^j) = 0. \tag{3.4}$$

For any given vector of local emission tax rates, $\vec{\tau} := (\tau^1, \ldots, \tau^n)^T$, the system of the $2n$ f.o.c.s, given by (3.3)–(3.4), determines firms' equilibrium output and emission levels, $\{Q^j(\vec{\tau}), E^j(\vec{\tau})\}_{j=1,\ldots,n}$.[8]

2.2 Consumers

Let local consumers' preferences for the private good be represented by monotonously decreasing local demand functions $d^j(p^j) \, \forall j = 1, \ldots, n$. Accordingly, let $p^j(q^j)$ denote the local inverse demand functions. Since in equilibrium no interregional arbitrage is possible, the price must be the same everywhere. Using the equilibrium condition $p^j = p^i \, \forall i, j$ and aggregating local demands, $D(p) := \sum_{j=1}^n d^j(p)$, we can derive the national inverse demand function P. From market clearing we know that demand equals supply,

$$D(p) = \sum_{j=1}^n q^j = \sum_{j=1}^n Q^j = Q,$$

where $q^j = d^j(p)$. Hence, local residents' consumer surplus is given by

$$\int_0^{q^j} p^j(\xi) d\xi - P(Q) q^j.$$

In each region, local residents hold all shares of the local firm and therefore gain its full profit. Furthermore, local residents benefit from the provision level of a local public good, G^j, which is financed by the revenue from local emission taxation, $\tau^j E^j$. We model the provision of local public goods as producing one unit of the public good by sacrificing one unit of a private good (namely, the numéraire). This means that we measure the supply of public goods by its cost. For tractability, we rule out interregional spillovers of local public goods, i.e., we deal with purely local public goods. (Non-residents are perfectly prevented from using local public goods of other regions at zero cost.)

On the other hand, residents suffer from industrial pollutant emission directly and indirectly: firstly, pollutant emissions impair the prevailing environmental quality; and secondly, they deteriorate the consumption conditions of public services by diminishing the use of a given provision level.[9] Let $E := \sum_{j=1}^n E^j$ denote total national pollutant emissions. The (composed) utility derived by residents of region j from the provision of the local public good and from aggregate emissions is denoted by $U^j(G^j, E)$.[10] We assume that U^j is monotonously increasing in G^j, monotonously decreasing in E, and concave in its arguments.[11] In total, the welfare of the residents in region j is equal to[12]

$$W^j(\vec{\tau}) = \int_0^{q^j} p^j(\xi)d\xi - P(Q)q^j + U^j(G^j, E) + \Pi^j(Q^j, E^j; Q^{-j}, \tau^j),$$

(3.5)

where the firm's profit is given by (3.2) and the public budget constraint equates revenue and spending, $G^j = \tau^j E^j$.

3 WELFARE ANALYSIS: NASH TAX RATES VERSUS COOPERATIVE TAX RATES

In this section we derive a Nash equilibrium of interjurisdictional tax competition, i.e., the optimal policy of each local government given the (optimal) tax rates of all other regions.[13] Afterwards, we examine how local governments set their tax rates if they behave cooperatively and compare these tax rates with their equilibrium levels. This enables us to discover the incentives that prompt local governments to deviate from the considered cooperative solution. But before turning to this, we have to investigate further the supply and emission level of a single firm and the corresponding aggregate values for any given vector of tax rates. Then, taking into account the market behaviour of the firms, each government determines its Nash tax rate, given the (equilibrium) tax rates of the remainder of the nation.[14]

3.1 Comparative Statics of Supply and Pollutant Emissions

Suppose that the local government of region j considers a change of its emission tax rate, τ^j. This policy measure directly affects the behaviour of the local firm, whose output decision, in turn, has an impact on the behaviour of all competitors. Hence, to evaluate the consequences of a change of the local emission tax, one needs to know the effect of τ^j on the market values of Q^j, E^j, Q^{-j}, E^{-j} ($E^{-j} := \sum_{i \neq j} E^i$), and thereby on its aggregates Q and E.

Evaluating any firm's f.o.c.s at some market equilibrium and differentiating (3.4) with respect to τ^j and solving for the derivatives $\partial E^i / \partial \tau^j$

yields

$$\frac{\partial E^i}{\partial \tau^j} = \begin{cases} -\dfrac{1 + C^j_{qe} Q^j_{\tau j}}{C^j_{ee}} & \text{for } i = j, \\[3mm] -\dfrac{C^i_{qe} Q^i_{\tau j}}{C^i_{ee}} & \text{for } i \neq j. \end{cases} \tag{3.6}$$

Analogously, differentiating (3.3) and using (3.6) yields

$$Q^j_{\tau j}\left(P' - \frac{1}{C^j_{ee}}\left(C^j_{qq}C^j_{ee} - C^{j^2}_{qe}\right)\right) + Q_{\tau j}(P' + P''Q^j) = -\frac{C^j_{qe}}{C^j_{ee}}, \tag{3.7}$$

$$Q^i_{\tau j}\left(P' - \frac{1}{C^i_{ee}}\left(C^i_{qq}C^i_{ee} - C^{i^2}_{qe}\right)\right) + Q_{\tau j}(P' + P''Q^i) = 0 \quad \forall i \neq j. \tag{3.8}$$

Note that the term $C^i_{qq}C^i_{ee} - C^{i^2}_{qe}$ is the determinant of the Hessian matrix of C^i which is by strict convexity positive $(det(Hess(C^i)) > 0)$.

Let $a^i := P' + P''Q^i < 0$ and $b^i := P' - [det(Hess(C^i))/C^i_{ee}] < 0$ $\forall i = 1, \ldots, n$. Solving (3.8) for $Q^i_{\tau j}$, summing over all $i \neq j$, using $Q_{\tau j} \equiv Q^j_{\tau j} + Q^{-j}_{\tau j}$, and solving for $Q^j_{\tau j}$ gives

$$Q^j_{\tau j} = \left(1 + \sum_{i \neq j} \frac{a^i}{b^i}\right) Q_{\tau j}.$$

Substituting into (3.7) and rearranging terms yields

$$Q^j_{\tau j} = -\frac{C^j_{qe}}{C^j_{ee}} \frac{1 + \sum_{i \neq j} \frac{a^i}{b^i}}{a^j + b^j\left(1 + \sum_{i \neq j} \frac{a^i}{b^i}\right)} < 0, \tag{3.9}$$

$$Q^{-j}_{\tau j} = \frac{C^j_{qe}}{C^j_{ee}} \frac{\sum_{i \neq j} \frac{a^i}{b^i}}{a^j + b^j\left(1 + \sum_{i \neq j} \frac{a^i}{b^i}\right)} > 0, \tag{3.10}$$

$$Q_{\tau j} = -\frac{C^j_{qe}}{C^j_{ee}} \frac{1}{a^j + b^j\left(1 + \sum_{i \neq j} \frac{a^i}{b^i}\right)} < 0. \tag{3.11}$$

If the government of region j increases its emission tax, the local firm responds to this by a decrease of its output, whereas non-resident firms raise their output quantities. Aggregating these variations we see that, although Q^{-j} increases, total supply decreases.

Substituting (3.9)–(3.11) into (3.6) gives us the signs of the variations of pollutant emissions:

$$E^j_{\tau^j} < 0, \qquad E^i_{\tau^j} > 0 \;\forall i \neq j, \qquad E^{-j}_{\tau^j} > 0. \qquad (3.12)$$

Analogously to (3.9) and (3.10), the use of environmental inputs decreases in jurisdiction j and increases in all other jurisdictions as τ^j increases. But contrary to Q_{τ^j}, and although we can unambiguously determine the signs of the derivatives of local pollutant emissions, we are not able to decide, in general, whether total emissions rise or fall. To see this, sum $E^i_{\tau^j}$ over all i. Using (3.9)–(3.11), we can write the derivative of total emissions as

$$E_{\tau^j} = -\left[\frac{1}{C^j_{ee}} + Q_{\tau^j} \left(\frac{C^j_{qe}}{C^j_{ee}} + \sum_{i \neq j} \left(\frac{C^j_{qe}}{C^j_{ee}} - \frac{C^i_{qe}}{C^i_{ee}} \right) \frac{a^i}{b^i} \right) \right]. \qquad (3.13)$$

Since we do not know whether the sum in (3.13) is positive or negative, the sign of E_{τ^j} is indeterminate.[15] For the special case of identical firms and equal tax rates in all jurisdictions, the sum term drops out and total emissions fall if one single government raises its tax rate. In particular, we get

$$E^j_{\tau^j} = -\left(\frac{1}{C_{ee}} + Q^j_{\tau^j} \frac{C_{qe}}{C_{ee}} \right) < 0, \qquad (3.14)$$

$$E^i_{\tau^j} = -\frac{1}{n-1} Q^{-j}_{\tau^j} \frac{C_{qe}}{C_{ee}} > 0 \qquad \forall i \neq j, \qquad (3.15)$$

$$E_{\tau^j} = -\left(\frac{1}{C_{ee}} + Q_{\tau^j} \frac{C_{qe}}{C_{ee}} \right) < 0. \qquad (3.16)$$

Correspondingly, the changes of the supplied quantities are given[16] by

$$Q^j_{\tau^j} = -\frac{C_{qe}}{C_{ee}} \frac{1}{b} \frac{(n-1)a+b}{na+b} < 0, \qquad (3.17)$$

$$Q^{-j}_{\tau^j} = \frac{C_{qe}}{C_{ee}} \frac{1}{b} \frac{(n-1)a}{na+b} > 0, \qquad (3.18)$$

$$Q_{\tau^j} = -\frac{C_{qe}}{C_{ee}} \frac{1}{b} \frac{b}{na+b} < 0, \qquad (3.19)$$

where $a = P' + P''Q/n$ and $b = P' - det(Hess(C))$.

In the special case of identical firms facing equal local emission tax rates, the change of one single tax rate has analogous effects on emission and output levels. Although an increase of τ^j induces all firms, except that of region j, to raise their emission and output levels, aggregate values decrease. Hence, supply and pollutant emissions move in the same direction.

3.2 Equilibrium of Interjurisdictional Tax Competition

Suppose that, for any vector of the other regions' tax rates, the local regulator of region j maximizes the welfare of her residents, given by (3.5), subject to the public budget constraint, $G^j = \tau^j E^j$, and the behaviour of the local firms, characterized by (3.3) and (3.4). Differentiating, for any given vector $(\tau^1, \ldots, \tau^{j-1}, \tau^{j+1}, \ldots, \tau^n)^T$, the welfare function, $\mathcal{W}^j$, with respect to τ^j yields

$$\mathcal{W}^j_{\tau^j}(\vec{\tau}) = U^j_e E_{\tau^j} + \left(U^j_g - 1\right) E^j + U^j_g \tau^j E^j_{\tau^j} - q^j P' Q_{\tau^j} + P' Q^j Q^{-j}_{\tau^j}. \tag{3.20}$$

Setting its derivative equal to zero, and solving[17] for τ^j leads to

$$\tau^j = -\frac{U^j_e}{U^j_g} \frac{E_{\tau^j}}{E^j_{\tau^j}} + \frac{1 - U^j_g}{U^j_g} \frac{E^j}{E^j_{\tau^j}} + \frac{q^j}{U^j_g} \frac{P'}{E^j_{\tau^j}} Q_{\tau^j} - \frac{1}{U^j_g} \frac{P'}{E^j_{\tau^j}} Q^j Q^{-j}_{\tau^j} \tag{3.21}$$

$$= -\frac{U^j_e}{U^j_g} \frac{E_{\tau^j}}{E^j_{\tau^j}} + \frac{1 - U^j_g}{U^j_g} \frac{E^j}{E^j_{\tau^j}} - \frac{P' Q_{\tau^j}}{U^j_g E^j_{\tau^j}} \left(Q^j - q^j\right) + \frac{P' Q^j Q^j_{\tau^j}}{U^j_g E^j_{\tau^j}}. \tag{3.22}$$

where $E_{\tau^j} = E^j_{\tau^j} + E^{-j}_{\tau^j}$. Because every local government $(j = 1, \ldots, n)$ adjusts its tax rate according to (3.21) (or (3.22)), the resulting, interdependent equation system determines the vector of equilibrium tax rates – the Nash equilibrium of interjurisdictional competition – as a fixed point.

The local emission tax consists of four parts: the first term of (3.21) (or (3.22)) reflects the fact that a rise of the local emission tax, τ^j, not only alters local pollutant emissions, E^j, but also the pollutant emissions of all non-resident firms. Hence, due to pollutant transmission, the local government has to evaluate the resulting *total* variation of E by multiplying marginal total emissions by local marginal social damage. From (3.12) we know that $E^{-j}_{\tau^j} > 0$ and $E^j_{\tau^j} < 0$, so that the total emission reduction, $-E_{\tau^j}$, falls short of local reduction, $E^j_{\tau^j}$. Therefore, the bracket term of the first part is smaller than unity, implying that the first part falls short of *local* marginal social damage.

The second term of (3.21) (or (3.22)) stems from distortionary tax-ation and reflects public financial needs. Since the tax basis (pollutant emissions) is under control of private agents, increasing the local tax rate induces a production shift towards the other regions. This widens, *ceteris paribus*, the foreign tax basis, resulting in a fiscal externality: the other regional governments gain by means of increased public revenues. If the local regulator were authorized to raise public funds through head taxes, this externality would be evaded and any public good would be provided at its efficient level, i.e., at that level where the marginal rate of trans-formation between the private and the public good equals the marginal rate of substitution between these two goods: $U_g^j = 1$. In this case, the second term of (3.21) drops out. If, however, local public goods are un-derprovided, $U_g^j > 1$, the sign of the second term is positive (and *vice versa*). Underprovision[18] of public goods, and thus a relative scarcity of public funds, encourages a further increase of the emission tax, whereas, on the contrary, overprovision discourages emission taxation. This fact is widely ignored in the environmental literature.[19]

The third term of (3.21) results from a change of local consumer sur-plus. Clearly, as we know from (3.11), a higher emission tax reduces total supply and thus consumer surplus; this causes the third term to be negative.

Since residents hold all shares of the local firm and therefore receive its full profit as dividend income, they bear the full amount of the local firm's cost resulting from a rise of the local emission tax. However, a tightening of the tax screw not only affects the behaviour of the local firm but also of non-resident firms. Hence, this policy measure has a twofold impact on local residents' dividend income: a *direct* and an *indirect* effect. The first is given by $\Pi_{\tau j}^j = -E^j < 0$, which is already taken into account by the second term of (3.21); the second, the indirect profit effect, is represented by the fourth term of (3.21), $\Pi_{q-j}^j Q_{\tau j}^{-j} = P'Q^j Q_{\tau j}^{-j}$, which is unambiguously negative. An increase of the local emission tax has a positive effect on the supply of non-resident firms and therefore a negative effect on the market price. Hence, the local firm's revenue and thus local consumers' dividend income decrease indirectly if the local regulator raises the emission tax.

Equivalently, writing τ^j in the form of (3.22) we get an alternative interpretation of the last two parts. (This formulation is closely related to the presentation commonly used in the literature.) In this case, the third part depends on local excess supply. If a region is a net exporter, the third part tends to increase the emissions tax (and *vice versa*). In international economics, this effect is called the *terms-of-trade effect*. (See, for example, Brander and Spencer, 1985.) If no other effects were present, the equilibrium tax rate of a net-exporting region would exceed local marginal damage. Hence, ignoring endogenous provision of public goods, non-competitive behaviour, and interregional pollutant transmission – as, for example, Krutilla (1991) and Pethig (1994) do – leads to the somehow ecologically 'euphoric' conclusion that interjurisdictional tax competition in emission taxes does not induce 'ecological dumping'[20] for exporting regions.

The fourth part of (3.22) stems from non-competitive behaviour of the firm of region j. To see this, recall that the fourth part of (3.21) reflects the effect of the induced change of Q^{-j} on the output price and thus on firm j's revenue. Since the non-competitive firm realizes its own impact on the equilibrium price and on its revenue, $P'Q^j dQ^j$ (see (3.3)), the welfare effect of τ^j on the firm's revenue through Q^j drops out by application of the envelope theorem. Hence, the remaining welfare effect that has to be considered by the local regulator results from the impact of the behaviour of the other competitors on the local firm's revenue through the market price, given by $P'Q^j Q_{\tau^j}^{-j}$. If, however, firm j behaved perfectly competitively, the regulator would also have to take into account this price effect by adding $P'Q^j Q_{\tau^j}^j$ to (3.20). In this case, the fourth part of (3.22) would drop out. Therefore, this term stems from non-competitive behaviour and reflects a local government's endeavour to make the resident firm behave as if it were a Stackelberg leader. (See, for example, Eaton and Grossman, 1986.)

Notice that as long as the local firm behaves non-competitively the sum of the third and the fourth part is unambiguously negative, which can easily be seen by inspection of (3.21). If, however, we discarded our assumption of non-competitive behaviour and assumed instead that the local firm behaves competitively, the local regulator would have to consider the term $-P'Q^j Q_{\tau^j}^j / (U_g^j E_{\tau^j}^j) > 0$ in (3.21). Since this results in a change of the tax formula, the sign of the sum of the last two parts of (3.21) becomes ambiguous. Namely, as we see from (3.22), its sign depends exclusively on local excess supply.[21]

Let us turn back to the case where firms behave non-competitively. Then the sum of the last two terms of (3.21) is negative, and we get the following result when pollution is non-transboundary:

Proposition 3.1 *Assume that pollutant emissions are purely local. The local emission tax exceeds (falls short of) local marginal environmental damage if, and only if, public funds are relatively scarce (not too scarce), in the sense that*

$$U_g^j - 1 \underset{(<)}{>} \frac{P'}{E^j} \left(q^j Q_{\tau^j} - Q^j Q_{\tau^j}^{-j} \right). \tag{3.23}$$

Proof: If there is no pollutant transmission, the total change of pollutants that affect local environmental quality equals $E_{\tau^j}^j$. In this case, the first term of the equilibrium tax rate, given by (3.21), reduces to $-U_e^j/U_g^j$. Then Proposition 3.1 follows directly from the tax formula. $\square$

As long as residents' marginal utility of the public good is not too high, the emission tax falls short of local marginal damage and therefore the environmental quality is too low. But if public services are underprovided to such a large extent that U_g^j, the marginal value of public funds, is sufficiently high, the government fixes τ^j above $-U_e^j/U_g^j$; in this case, environmental quality is too high(!) rather than too low.

Note that the right hand side of (3.23) can also be written as

$$P' \frac{Q^j}{E^j} Q_{\tau^j} \left(\frac{Q_{\tau^j}^j}{Q_{\tau^j}} - \frac{Q^j - q^j}{Q^j} \right).$$

Since $Q_{\tau^j}^j/Q_{\tau^j}$ is larger but $(Q^j - q^j)/Q^j$ is lower than one, the bracket term is positive; and, therefore, the right hand side of (3.23) is also positive, implying that the sum of the third and the fourth part of (3.21) is negative. Hence, τ^j can only exceed marginal damage if $U_g^j - 1 > 0$ (underprovision of public goods); conversely, if $U_g^j - 1 < 0$ (overprovision of public goods), then the emission tax must fall short of marginal damage. As long as residents' marginal utility of public goods, U_g^j, is not too high, the emission tax falls short of local marginal damage and, therefore, the environmental quality is too low. But if public services are underprovided to such a large extent that U_g^j is sufficiently high, the government fixes τ^j above $-U_e^j/U_g^j$; in this case, environmental quality is too high(!) rather than too low. Thus, even if pollution is purely

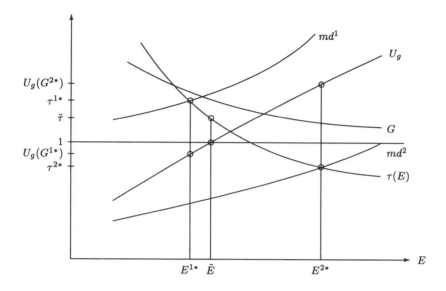

Figure 3.1: The optimal tax rate

local, tax competition leads to 'ecological dumping' if there are no severe financial needs of the public sector. However, in a polar case, the
government may also 'overtax' pollutant emissions if fiscal aspects dominate environmental and trade-strategic aspects.[22] Hence, if pollution is
purely local, one of the following three regimes emerges, depending on
the steepness of the social damage curve and on the curvature of the
(inverse) demand curve for environmental inputs. (The interdependence
between the environmental quality and the provision level of public services is also depicted in Figure 3.1, where $\tau(E)$ represents the inverse
demand curve for environmental inputs, i.e., the maximum price firms
are willing to pay for the right to pollute.)

Regime 1: The damage curve is sufficiently steep that the potential tax
revenue that would result from the Pigouvian tax ($\tau^* = -U_e/U_g =:$
md) – the point where the marginal damage curve, md, and the indirect demand curve, $\tau(E)$, intersect – exceeds the yield necessary
to provide public services efficiently. Consider Figure 3.1. If the
relevant social marginal damage curve is md^1, the Pigouvian tax
τ^{1*} would collect a public revenue equal to $\tau^{1*}E^{1*}$, leading to over-

provision of public services, $(U_g(G^{1*}) < 1)$.[23] To avoid excessive overprovision and to promote the local industry, the government gives the firms a tax relief by adjusting the emission tax below the Pigouvian level: $\tilde{\tau} < \tau < \tau^{1*})$. Yet, public services are still overprovided(!) while the environmental quality is too low.

Regime 2: In this case, the marginal damage curve exhibits some moderate steepness in the following sense. The Pigouvian emission tax would yield public funds that either exceed or fall short of the revenue needed to provide public services efficiently. However, strategic effects prompt the government to decrease the emission tax, resulting in a public revenue that is not sufficient to provide the efficient amount of public services. Therefore, the provision level of public services and environmental quality are too low. In Figure 3.1, this occurs if the government fixes its emission tax below $\tilde{\tau}$, if md^1 applies, and below τ^{2*}, if md^2 applies.

Regime 3: Here the damage curve is sufficiently flat (md^2 applies) such that the potential revenue stemming from the Pigouvian tax $(\tau^{2*}E^{2*})$ does not enable the government to provide public services efficiently, $(U_g(G^{2*}) > 1)$. The tax revenue is even so low that the government, in spite of the prevailing trade effects, decides to impose an emission tax exceeding marginal damage $(\tau^2 > \tau^{2*})$; however, the regulator does not increase the tax rate up to the point where public services can be provided efficiently $(\tau^2 = \tilde{\tau})$. Hence, we have underprovision of public services but a too high(!) environmental quality.

We see that, depending on the steepness of the social damage curve, one out of three regimes occurs: if marginal damage is high (e.g., md^1), the optimal tax never exceeds its Pigouvian level (τ^{1*}) since this would imply overprovision of public services and simultaneously a too high environmental quality. Thus, for relatively steep damage curves we have a too low environmental quality and, depending on the significance of the strategic effects, either overprovision $(\tau^1 \in (\tilde{\tau}; \tau^{1*}))$ or underprovision of public services $(\tau^1 < \tilde{\tau})$. If, however, the social damage curve is relatively flat (e.g., md^2 applies), the government fixes its emission tax beneath the level sufficient to provide public services efficiently $(\tilde{\tau})$, resulting in underprovision of public services and either a too high environmental quality ($\tau^2 \in (\tau^{2*}; \tilde{\tau})$) or a too low environmental quality ($\tau^2 < \tau^{2*}$). We condense these findings in the following proposition.[24]

Proposition 3.2 *If the social damage curve is sufficiently steep (flat), public services are overprovided (underprovided) but the environmental quality is too low (high). In the intermediate case, the provision level of public services and the environmental quality are too low.*

Surprisingly, in two out of three cases either public services are overprovided or the environmental quality is too high. Only in the second regime do we get the commonly expected result that interjurisdictional tax competition leads to underprovision of public goods and to a too low environmental quality. The reason that this does not necessarily occur – and we will see that it may even be impossible(!) – is that the emission tax crucially depends on the social value of public funds. This interdependence between the provision level of public services and the prevailing environmental quality drives our results.

Note that these findings include a wide range of special cases. In particular, our results are (also) true if firms behave perfectly competitively, if local demand equals zero (pure export industry), or if the trade balance is settled ($q^j = Q^j$).[25] Moreover, even in the case where pollutants are perfectly transboundary, we cannot rule out that emission taxes are set above marginal damage.[26] If the social damage curve is sufficiently flat, $\tau^j > -U_e^j / U_g^j$ may occur, although pollution is transboundary. Hence, a generalization of Conrad's (1993) result (p. 128), who finds that under imperfect competition pollution taxes are set below local marginal damage, is not possible if we take into account strategic effects and governmental financial needs; nor does the classical result of regional economics, that interjurisdictional tax competition leads to underprovision of public goods,[27] necessarily remain valid if we consider environmental aspects and allow for emission taxation. Rather, including endogenous provision of public goods, environmental policy, and strategic trade policy in one model, interjurisdictional tax competition may – in polar cases – result either in overprovision of public services or in a too high environmental quality.[28]

Identical regions

To gain even more definitive results, consider the special case of identical regions in the following. Assume that in all regions firms exhibit the same technologies and consumers have the same preferences, $U^j = U^i = U$ and $d^j = d^i \, \forall i, j$. Focusing on a symmetric equilibrium, i.e., $\tau^i = \tau^j \, \forall i, j$, the profit-maximizing production decisions are the same for all firms: $E^j = E/n$ and $Q^j = Q/n \, \forall j$; and, similarly, the tax rates affect aggregate values symmetrically: $Q_{\tau^j} = Q_{\tau^i}$, $E_{\tau^j} = E_{\tau^i}$, $Q_{\tau^j}^{-j} = Q_{\tau^i}^{-i}$, and $E_{\tau^j}^{-j} = E_{\tau^i}^{-i} \, \forall i, j$. In this case, (3.20) reduces to

$$W_{\tau^j}^j = U_e E_{\tau^j} + (U_g - 1) \frac{E}{n} + U_g \tau^j E_{\tau^j}^j - \frac{Q}{n} P' Q_{\tau^j}^j. \qquad (3.24)$$

Setting this equal to zero and solving for τ^j yields the Nash tax rates of a symmetric equilibrium,

$$\tau^j = -\frac{U_e}{U_g} \frac{E_{\tau^j}}{E_{\tau^j}^j} + \frac{1 - U_g}{U_g} \frac{E/n}{E_{\tau^j}^j} + \frac{P'Q/n}{U_g} \frac{Q_{\tau^j}^j}{E_{\tau^j}^j} \qquad \forall j. \qquad (3.25)$$

For identical regions local excess supply equals zero, i.e., there is no interregional trade and thus no terms-of-trade effect. In this case, the third part of (3.22) drops out, and the remaining strategic term stems from imperfect competition and interregional pollutant transmission. If, in addition, firms behave perfectly competitively and pollutants are purely local (no pollutant transmission) we have the following proposition.

Proposition 3.3 *If pollution is purely local and firms behave perfectly competitively, a local government fixes its tax rate above (beneath) marginal damage if, and only if, public goods are underprovided (overprovided).*

Proposition 3.3 reveals the presence of a strong link between environmental quality and the provision of public goods. In the special case of purely local pollution and perfectly competitive firms, we have either overprovision of public services and a too low environmental quality or the opposite holds. Hence, under these circumstances, either the classical result of regional economics (underprovision of public goods) or environmental economists' fear that interjurisdictional tax competition leads to a too lax environmental policy is wrong.

If, however, lump sum transfers and head taxes are available, which is often (implicitly) assumed in the literature, the local government can provide public services efficiently. Then (3.25) reduces to[29]

$$\tau^j = -U_e + \frac{P'Q}{n}\frac{Q^j_{\tau^j}}{E^j_{\tau^j}} \qquad \forall j. \tag{3.26}$$

If, in addition, firms behave perfectly competitively we have the following proposition.[30]

Proposition 3.4 *If pollution is purely local, firms behave perfectly competitively, and the social value of public funds equals private marginal utility of income, interjurisdictional competition in emission tax rates is efficient, i.e., the equilibrium emission tax rates equal the Pigouvian emission taxes.*

Proposition 3.4 states that, only in a special limiting case, interjurisdictional tax competition in emission taxes leads to efficiency. Since, in general, we have to expect inefficiency, this result is rather discouraging. However, provided that efficiency is not an equilibrium outcome, the situation can be improved if, instead of engaging in interjurisdictional competition, (local) governments determine their emission tax rates cooperatively by maximizing the overall welfare with respect to all tax rates simultaneously. Given their limited policy tools, this measure allows them to achieve a second-best allocation. Unfortunately, the considered cooperative solution is not an equilibrium, in general. To investigate the incentives that prompt local governments to deviate from this second-best solution, we derive the cooperative emission tax rates and compare them with their equilibrium values in the next section.

3.3 Cooperative Behaviour of Local Governments

Let local governments behave cooperatively in the sense that they maximize the sum of all local welfare functions with respect to the emission taxes. Using the market-clearing condition and substituting profit terms, given by (3.2), into (3.5) yields the cooperative maximization problem

$$\max_{\vec{\tau}} \sum_{i=1}^n \mathcal{W}^i(\vec{\tau}) = \int_0^Q P(\xi)d\xi + \sum_{i=1}^n U^i(G^i, E) - \sum_{i=1}^n \left(C^i(Q^i, E^i) + \tau^i E^i\right). \tag{3.27}$$

Setting its derivatives equal to zero and rearranging terms yields

$$-P' \sum_{i=1}^{n} Q^i Q^i_{\tau j} + \sum_{i=1}^{n} \tau^i U^i_g E^i_{\tau j} + E_{\tau j} \sum_{i=1}^{n} U^i_e - (1-U^j_g)E^j = 0, \qquad \forall j.$$

(3.28)

Let $\tilde{D}_e := -\sum_i U^i_e$, $R^i_{\tau j} := P'Q^i Q^i_{\tau j}$, and let $J\vec{E}(\vec{\tau})$ denote the Jacobian matrix of $\vec{E} := (E^1, \ldots, E^n)^T$. Additionally defining[31]

$$\tilde{U}_g := \begin{bmatrix} U^1_g & & 0 \\ & \ddots & \\ 0 & & U^n_g \end{bmatrix} \quad \text{and} \quad \vec{R}_{\vec{\tau}} := \begin{bmatrix} \sum_i R^i_{\tau 1} \\ \vdots \\ \sum_i R^i_{\tau n} \end{bmatrix},$$

we can write the equation system (3.28) in matrix notation as

$$-\vec{R}_{\vec{\tau}} - \left(I_n - \tilde{U}_g\right)\vec{E} + J\vec{E}(\vec{\tau})^T \tilde{U}_g \vec{\tau} - \tilde{D}_e J\vec{E}(\vec{\tau})^T \iota_n = 0, \qquad (3.29)$$

where I_n denotes the identity matrix of rank n and $\iota_n := (1, \ldots, 1)^T$. Solving (3.29) for $\vec{\tau}$ yields[32]

$$\vec{\tau} = \tilde{U}_g^{-1} \left(\tilde{D}_e \iota_n + \left(J\vec{E}(\vec{\tau})^T\right)^{-1} \left(\left(I_n - \tilde{U}_g\right)\vec{E} + \vec{R}_{\vec{\tau}}\right)\right). \qquad (3.30)$$

The optimal cooperative tax rates, determined by equation system (3.30), consist of three additive terms. The first term, $-\sum_i U^i_e/U^j_g$, reflects the *overall* social marginal damage of pollutant emissions, which is clearly higher than pure local damage, $-U^j_e/U^j_g$. In addition, the marginal environmental damage is multiplied by unity in the cooperative tax rate formula, whereas it is multiplied by $1 + (E^{-j}_{\tau j}/E^j_{\tau j}) < 1$ in the competitive case (see (3.21)). Thus, there are at least two *environmental externalities* which cause the equilibrium tax rates to fall short of social environmental damage associated with one additional unit of pollutant emission: firstly, the neglect of overall environmental damages, i.e., real externalities resulting from local emissions; and secondly, the strategic effect of increased pollutant emissions in all other regions, diminishing the benefit from local pollutant reduction through interregional pollutant transmission. Clearly, both effects are due to transboundary pollution and vanish if pollution is purely local.

In contrast to the (non-cooperative) equilibrium taxes, the (cooperative) second-best tax rates also take into account the *fiscal externalities* on public revenues of the other jurisdictions, $J\vec{E}(\vec{\tau})'^{-1}(I_n - \tilde{U}_g)\vec{E}$. The direct increase of local public revenue resulting from a rise of the emission tax, E^j, is multiplied by the wedge between marginal utility of private income and the social value of public funds, $1 - U_g^j$, and weighted by the variation of all local emissions, the inverse Jacobian matrix of E.[33]

All income effects accruing to consumers through their dividend receipts are reflected by the third part of (3.30), $J\vec{E}(\vec{\tau})'^{-1}\vec{R}_{\vec{\tau}}$. Contrary to the Nash taxes, which only account for local effects, the cooperative tax rates encompass *all* cross-revenue effects resulting from the compound effects of output changes, $\sum_i P'(Q)Q^i Q_{\tau^j}^i$, and overall variations of emission demands, $J\vec{E}(\vec{\tau})$. Since these *income externalities* are due to imperfect competition on the output market, the third part of (3.30) vanishes if firms behave perfectly competitively.

In sum, the cooperative tax rates reflect all interregional effects; that is, they correct for (direct and indirect) environmental, fiscal, and income externalities. Moreover, condensing our observations, the cooperative tax rates are given by

$$\tau^j = -\frac{U_e^j}{U_g^j} + \frac{1}{U_g^j}\left(J\vec{E}(\vec{\tau})^T\right)_{jj}^{-1}\left(1 - U_g^j\right)E^j \qquad \forall j \qquad (3.31)$$

if firms behave perfectly competitively and pollution is non-transboundary, where $(J\vec{E}(\vec{\tau})^T)_{jj}^{-1}$ denotes the j,j element of the inverse of the Jacobian of $\vec{E}$. Equation (3.31) gives us the next proposition.

Proposition 3.5 *Let firms behave perfectly competitively and let pollution be purely local. The cooperative tax rate of region j exceeds (falls short of) marginal damage if, and only if, public goods are underprovided (overprovided).*

As in the Nash equilibrium, governments try to weigh the trade-off between providing a better environmental quality, raising public funds, and encouraging economic activities. When governments set their tax rates cooperatively, we have, in general, either overprovision of public services and an inefficient low environmental quality, or the environmental quality is too high but public services are underprovided.[34]

After having derived the Nash and the second-best tax rates, the question arises whether the former fall short of the latter. Although one may presume that the Nash tax rates are too low, little can be said in general. However, for the special case of two regions where firms behave competitively and pollution is non-transboundary we have the following proposition.

Proposition 3.6 *Let firms behave perfectly competitively and let pollution be purely local. In the special case of two regions, local governments fix their equilibrium tax rates too low (high) if, in equilibrium, we have underprovision (overprovision) of public goods in both jurisdictions.*

Proof: Proposition 3.6 is easily proved by applying (3.30) to the special case of two regions and comparing the result with the equilibrium tax rates, given by (3.21). □

Proposition 3.6 states that if no strategic effects are present and if, in both regions, public revenue falls short of the expenditure required to provide public services efficiently, equilibrium tax rates are fixed below their second-best levels (and *vice versa*). The intuition behind this is the following. Local governments do not consider the induced fiscal externalities resulting from determination of their tax rates. If one region raises its emission tax, the emissions and thereby the tax revenue of the other region increase. Hence, the other region gains from this policy measure (in terms of public revenue) if local public goods are underprovided; but loses if local public goods are overprovided. However, in the hybrid case where we have underprovision in one and overprovision in the other region, little can be said, in general; the same is true if we have more than two jurisdictions.

Identical regions

Again, to obtain more stringent results, consider a state (union) consisting of identical regions. In this case, the tax formula of the cooperative solution, (3.30), reduces to a quite simple one; by symmetry, we have[35]

$$\tau^j = -\frac{nU_e}{U_g} + \frac{1-U_g}{U_g}\frac{E/n}{E_{\tau^j}} + \frac{P'Q/n}{U_g}\frac{Q_{\tau^j}}{E_{\tau^j}} \qquad \forall j. \qquad (3.32)$$

In the symmetric case, each cooperative tax rate reflects the *nationwide* marginal environmental damage of local pollutant emissions which is, due to (perfect) pollutant transmission, nothing but n times local marginal damage. Note that formula (3.32) not (only) reflects the impact of τ^j on local pollutant emissions, $E_{\tau^j}^j$ – as it is the case in the formula of Nash tax rates, (3.25) – but also its overall impact, E_{τ^j}. Similarly, the last part of the right hand side of (3.32) includes the induced output changes of *all* firms, Q_{τ^j} – and not only of the local one, $Q_{\tau^j}^j$.[36]

3.4 The Sources of Inefficiency

In the preceding sections we have derived the equilibrium tax rates and the corresponding cooperative levels. It was indicated that both do not coincide, in general, because local governments neglect the external effects of their policy measures. In this section, we investigate in more detail the sources of this inefficiency, i.e., the motives that prompt local governments to deviate from a cooperative solution. To see how non-internalized effects distort second-best efficiency, it is expedient to consider the case of identical regions first, for little can be said if regions are heterogeneous.

To examine the unilateral incentive of jurisdiction j to deviate from the cooperative solution, we evaluate $\mathcal{W}_{\tau^j}^j$, (3.20), at the vector of the cooperative tax rates, (implicitly) given by (3.32). For illustrative purposes, it is instructive to subtract $\partial \sum_i \mathcal{W}^i / \partial \tau^j$, given by (3.28); a quantity which is, evaluated at the cooperative tax rates, equal to zero. Cancelling terms, this procedure yields

$$\mathcal{W}_{\tau^j}^j = -(n-1)U_e E_{\tau^j} - U_g \tau^j E_{\tau^j}^{-j} + \frac{Q}{n} P' Q_{\cdot j}^{-j}. \qquad (3.\bar{\ })$$

Three factors may prompt local governments to deviate from cooperative behaviour: the first term represents the *external marginal environmental damage* resulting from the overall variation of industrial pollutant emissions. Using $E_{\tau^j} = E_{\tau^j}^j + E_{\tau^j}^{-j}$, we see that, due to perfect pollutant transmission, this total non-internalized environmental damage consists of two parts: firstly, a change of local emissions directly affects the environmental quality of all other regions (*direct externality*); secondly, a rise of τ^j induces an increase of the emissions of non-resident firms equal to $E_{\tau^j}^{-j}$, causing additional environmental damage in all other regions (*indirect externality*). If, however, pollution is not perfectly transboundary, a third effect (a strategic effect) appears, which Kennedy (1994) calls the *pollution shifting effect*. If only some portion of the pollutant emissions abroad affects the environmental quality in the home region, a government may wish to shift production from home to abroad, for this improves the local environmental quality.

The second source of inefficiency stems from non-internalized *fiscal externalities* represented by the second term of (3.33). Although pollution shifting causes environmental external damages, it also induces external benefits. The induced increase of the emissions of non-resident firms, $E_{\tau^j}^{-j}$, results in a collection of additional public funds by other governments, given their tax rates. Multiplying these additional funds by their social price, U_g, gives the total external *fiscal effect*.

The third distorting effect originates from *production shifting*. A rise of the local emission tax, τ^j, not only affects the emissions but also the output quantities of all firms. Hence, consumer surplus and the local firm's profit vary in region j, but also in all other regions $i \neq j$. Accordingly, the third term of (3.33) splits up (additively) into a *consumption* and a *profit effect* (or *capital income effect*), given by $-\sum_{i\neq j} \frac{1}{n} P'QQ_{\tau^j}$ and $\sum_{i\neq j} P'Q^i Q_{\tau^j}^{-i}$, respectively.

Note that for competitive firms the third term of (3.33) drops out, since the first term of (3.28) vanishes and in (3.20) the last two terms are replaced by $-q^j P'Q_{\tau^j} + P'Q^j Q_{\tau^j} = P'(Q^j - q^j)Q_{\tau^j}$.

Thus far, we have interpreted the single terms of (3.33) which determine a local government's incentive to deviate from cooperative tax rates; yet, the sign of $W_{\tau^j}^j$ must be determined. Using (3.16) we see that the first term, stemming from *external marginal environmental damage*, is negative; from (3.15) we know that the second term, the *fiscal effect*, is also negative; and by (3.18) it is clear that the third distorting effect, the *production shifting effect*, is negative as well. Hence, all effects work in the same direction and the composite effect is definitely negative.

Proposition 3.7 *If all regions are identical and pollution is transboundary, each local government faces an unambiguous incentive to deviate from the cooperative solution by lowering its emission tax.*

If, however, pollution is non-transboundary, local emissions do not create external environmental effects stemming from pollutant transmission. Therefore, the direct and the indirect effect vanish. However, when pollution becomes incompletely transboundary the (strategic) pollution shifting effect becomes effective. This effect is positive, for local governments face some 'not-in-my-backyard' argument, which makes them fix their pollution taxes too high in order to drive out dirty production. (Everybody wants the good to be produced but nobody wants it to be produced in its own region.)

For the special case of competitive firms, we have a very comprehensible result.

Corollary 3.1 *If all regions are identical, pollution is purely local, and firms behave perfectly competitively, local governments set their emission tax rates too low (high) if, and only if, local public goods are underprovided (overprovided) in equilibrium.*

Proof: In the case of purely local pollution and perfectly competitive firms, (3.33) reduces to

$$W^j_{\tau j} = -(U_e + \tau U_g) E^{-j}_{\tau j},$$

which is negative if, and only if, $\tau > -U_e/U_g$. However, from (3.25) we know that if local firms behave competitively, $W^j_{\tau j} < 0$ is equivalent to $1 - U_g < 0$. This completes the proof of Corollary 3.1. □

Note that the incentive to deviate from cooperative tax rates may be ambiguous if jurisdictions are not identical, although the same effects as depicted above are present. To see this, consider the local government's incentive to deviate from cooperative tax rates in the general case:

$$W^j_{\tau j} = -E_{\tau j} \sum_{i \neq j} U^i_e - \sum_{i \neq j} U^i_g \tau^i E^i_{\tau j} + P' \sum_{i \neq j} Q^i Q^i_{\tau j} + (Q^j - q^j) P' Q_{\tau j}.$$

$$(3.34)$$

From (3.34) we see that we cannot derive a result similar to Proposition 3.7 for heterogeneous jurisdictions, because we cannot uniquely determine the sign of the right hand side. The reason for this is twofold. Firstly, for different regions, as we know from (3.13), the sign of $E_{\tau j}$ may either be positive or negative, i.e., it is not certain that the negative pollutant transmission effect dominates the positive pollution shifting effect. If the latter is sufficiently strong, the composite effect is positive, for non-resident firms extend pollutant emissions by more than the local firm reduces them. If this is the case, the external environmental effect provides some incentive to increase the emission tax.

Secondly, although the third term, which stems from non-competitive behaviour of local firms, is negative, it is not quite clear whether the sum of the last two strategic terms is negative as well. Since the last term depends on local excess supply, it is positive for 'exporting' and negative for 'importing' regions. Thus, the sum of these strategic effects is negative for regions exhibiting local excess demand and ambiguous for regions with local excess supply.

Therefore, in extreme cases, a local government's incentive to deviate from the considered cooperative solution, given by (3.34), *may* become positive. If, for example, region j encompasses so few consumers that q^j/Q tends to zero, and if the market share of firm j is sufficiently large, in the sense that $Q^j/Q > -\sum_{i \neq j}(Q^i/Q)(Q_{\tau j}^i/Q_{\tau j})$, the production shifting effect is positive. Clearly, if local consumers do not consume the considered item at all, $q^j = 0$, they are more concerned about profit income than about consumer surplus. (An objective function of this kind is analysed, for example, by Conrad, 1993.) By neglecting the latter they prefer lower output quantities and higher profits. In the limiting case, they advocate monopoly quantities and prices to exploit non-resident consumers totally. Under these conditions – provided that the environmental as well as the fiscal effect are not too strong – the local regulator determines the emission tax too high rather than too low.

Nevertheless, provided that the external environmental effect is negative, not only excess-demanding but also excess-supplying regions tax emissions too low, as long as their 'trade surplus' is not too large. In other words, only the small group of those regions that exhibit a sufficiently large excess supply does not tax emission too low.

To sum up, the analysis of this section emphasizes our previous result that an equilibrium is only efficient in a very limiting case, namely, when pollution is purely local, firms behave perfectly competitively, and the social value of public funds equals private marginal utility of income. (See note 25 and Proposition 3.4.) Conversely, the higher the (potential) externalities, the greater the incentives to deviate from second-best tax rates: the more pollutants are transboundary, public goods are provided at inefficient levels, and firms exert market power, the more a government is tempted to defect from environmental cooperation. Moreover, the analysis for the case of heterogeneous regions indicates that governments probably tax emissions too low rather than too high. Thus, our findings support rather than refute the thesis that interjurisdictional tax competition leads to 'ecological dumping'.

4 CONCLUDING REMARKS

We have elaborated a partial model of interjurisdictional tax competition encompassing environmental quality and the provision of a local public good. Each local government has to determine its emission tax rate which serves the threefold purpose of raising public funds, regulating emissions, and affecting the output market. The resulting equilibrium tax rates are contrasted with their cooperative, i.e., second-best, levels. We have identified three main factors that cause the equilibrium tax rates to differ from their efficient counterparts: firstly, an environmental effect, which can be decomposed into a direct, an indirect, and a pollution shifting effect; secondly, a fiscal effect resulting from the fact that governments are restricted to distortionary taxation; and thirdly, a production effect which can be split either into a change of consumer surplus and profit (dividend income) or, alternatively, into an imperfect competition and a terms-of-trade effect.

It is often stated that interjurisdictional tax competition leads to too low taxes on pollutant emissions if firms behave non-competitively. However, due to the strong link between environmental and fiscal policy, this need not be true, in general. If, in equilibrium, public funds are sufficiently scarce, i.e., public goods are underprovided to a large extent, the emission tax exceeds local marginal environmental damage. More precisely, if the social damage curve is sufficiently steep (flat), public services are overprovided (underprovided) while the environmental quality is too low (high). This implies that three possible cases may occur: in the two polar cases either public services are overprovided or the environmental quality is too high. Only in the intermediate regime do we get the common result of underprovision of public goods and a too low environmental quality. Moreover, we have shown that if, in the case of two jurisdictions, neither a strategic effect nor an external environmental damage effect is present, local governments fix their tax rates too low (high) if, in equilibrium, underprovision (overprovision) occurs in both regions. We have an even stronger result if regions are identical: provided that pollution is purely local and firms behave perfectly competitively, the emission tax exceeds marginal damage if, and only if, public goods are underprovided. Thus, in this case we have either a too high environmental quality or public services are overprovided.

Beyond this, for identical regions, each local government faces an incentive to deviate from the proposed cooperative solution (second-best tax rates) by lowering its tax rate. However, in the general case where jurisdictions are heterogeneous, we cannot exclude the possibility that some local governments attempt to deviate by increasing their tax rates. In particular, this may be the case if a local government is little concerned about consumer surplus and if nation-wide emissions increase as the local tax rate is raised. Nevertheless, it should be stressed that a positive incentive to deviate seems to be a more or less pathological case, for the fiscal effect gives a local government a strong incentive to fix its tax rate too low, rather than too high. Thus, the result found in the case of identical jurisdictions suggests that, as long as competing jurisdictions are 'almost' identical, every region attempts to undercut its cooperative tax rate. This gives us reason to support (weakly) the thesis that inter-jurisdictional tax competition leads to 'ecological dumping', though in some extreme cases environmental quality may be too high.

NOTES

1. This commonly made assumption of partial analysis implies that local governments have unlimited access to head taxation and thereby can provide local public goods efficiently.
2. Many authors restrict their analysis by assuming identical firms and/or countries (e.g., Kennedy, 1994).
3. Most authors assume that pollutant emissions depend directly on output. (See, for example, Ebert, 1992, and Kennedy, 1994.) We do not demand this but allow for 'separate' emission and output decisions.
4. Since the number of firms equals the number of jurisdictions, we implicitly assume that the total number of competing firms is exogenously fixed and not too large. The entry of new firms may be prevented by prohibitively high fixed costs which are already endured by the established firms. Requate (1994) considers an endogenous number of firms where all firms reside in one jurisdiction, whereas Markusen, Morey, and Olewiler (1993) scrutinize a model where the number and the location of plants is endogenous.
5. Subindices of functions denote partial derivatives unless stated otherwise.
6. This condition is slightly stronger than the one which is sufficient to ensure the concavity of the profit, $P''(Q) \leq -2P'(Q)/Q$.

7. Since this implies that the profit functions are also quasi-concave, the existence and uniqueness of a market equilibrium are guaranteed. (See, for example, Frank and Quandt, 1963 and Friedman, 1977, ch. 7, sec. 6.)

8. From now on, we denote by $Q^1, \ldots, Q^n$ and $E^1, \ldots, E^n$ the *equilibrium* values, implicitly given by firms' first-order conditions. Keeping this in mind, we do not refer to them as equilibrium values explicitly in the ensuing analysis, though we always consider these variables along the equilibrium path of the good market. Using this convention, we unambiguously attach the word 'equilibrium' to the outcome of interjurisdictional competition and the related variables.

9. For example, a visitor's utility derived from the consumption of a recreation area may depend on the levels of air and noise pollution.

10. This specification implies that pollutant transmission is perfectly transboundary, in general.

11. Alternatively, the function U^j can be interpreted as the social evaluation of public funds dependent on environmental quality.

12. Using an additively separable welfare function is very common in the international trade literature (e.g., Dixit, 1984, Brander and Spencer, 1985, and Eaton and Grossman, 1986) as well as in environmental economics (e.g., Krutilla, 1991, Conrad, 1993, and Kennedy, 1994). The implied absence of income effects is not essential for our results.

13. Unfortunately, we are not able to prove the existence and uniqueness of an equilibrium, in general. Indeed, the existence of a Nash equilibrium of interjurisdictional competition has turned out to be a problem in regional economics. (See, for example, Mintz and Tulkens, 1986.) A sufficient condition for the existence of a symmetric equilibrium is that the reaction curves are continuous and non-increasing. While the first property is guaranteed by the continuity of the factor demand functions and of the subutility function U, we cannot rule out (at least partially) increasing reaction curves, in general. Hence, all statements regarding any equilibrium are of the kind *'Provided that an equilibrium exists, the following is true ...'*.

14. We may view our game as a sequential game where, in the first stage, governments engage in tax competition and, in the second stage, firms play a Cournot game on the output market. Hence, we focus on subgame perfect equilibria.

15. This is consistent with Levin (1985) who finds that for uniform tax treatment of all firms the introduction of an emission tax may increase aggregate pollution if, roughly speaking, firms are sufficiently heterogeneous.

16. The results of Requate (1994) who considers a *single* regulator setting a

uniform emission tax for all firms remain true in a more general framework with firms residing in different jurisdictions. (Similarly, Conrad and Wang, 1993, find that for any of the three considered market structures aggregate output and pollution fall.)

17. Clearly, the phrase 'solving' is slightly inaccurate here, as well as in its subsequent use, since the right hand side still incorporates terms that depend on τ^j.

18. In fact, since the tax rate determines public revenue and spending, the provision level of the public good is endogenous. Thus, it should be kept in mind that whether public goods are under- or overprovided is not exogenous but an endogenous matter of fact.

19. Note that all effects are evaluated in terms of marginal utility of the local public good, i.e., in terms of marginal cost of public funds.

20. Following Rauscher (1994), Pethig (1994), and others, the phrase 'ecological dumping' does not mean price differentiation between home and abroad but '[...] a situation in which a government uses lax environmental standards to support domestic firms in international markets.' (Rauscher, 1994, p. 823.) For a discussion of the traditional notion of 'dumping' see, for example, Ethier (1982) and Davies and McGuinness (1982).

21. Evaluating (3.22) for a competitive firm at $U_g^j = 1$, we get the result of Krutilla (1991) and Pethig (1994).

22. This argument only makes sense if the government faces an increasing section of its Laffer curve, i.e., if $\partial G^j / \partial \tau^j = E^j + \tau^j (\partial E^j / \partial \tau^j) > 0$, which seems to be the most sensible assumption. In particular, we have not found any example where a government faces, in some relevant range, a decreasing section of the Laffer curve.

23. Note that, over the whole relevant range, the government faces an increasing Laffer curve $(\partial G^j / \partial \tau^j = E^j + \tau^j (\partial E^j / \partial \tau^j) > 0)$, i.e., the revenue curve is downward sloping in the E-τ diagram whereas the U_g curve is upward sloping.

24. Within a completely different model, Rauscher (1995) also emphasizes the dependence of the optimal emission tax on the steepness of the social damage curve.

25. Only for the special case where (i) pollution is purely local, (ii) firms behave perfectly competitively, (iii) revenues can be transferred to households (no or efficient provision of public goods), and (iv) trade does not occur, do local governments determine their emission tax rates (or pollution rights) efficiently. (See Wellisch, 1995, Proposition 3 therein.)

26. Note that, if the emission tax falls short of *local* marginal damage, it falls short of *nation-wide* marginal damage, all the more. Only if pollution is

purely local, do local and nation-wide marginal social damage coincide.

27. See, for example, Zodrow and Mieszkowski (1986), Wildasin (1988), and Bucovetsky and Wilson (1991).

28. The possibility that interjurisdictional tax competition may lead to over-provision of public goods was previously stressed by Wilson (1986). Moreover, some authors perceive that governments may have, for various reasons, an incentive to pursue a too stringent environmental policy. See, for example, Requate (1994), who considers an endogenous number of firms which are subject to a uniform emission tax, or Markusen (1975), Krutilla (1991), Barrett (1994), Rauscher (1995), and Ulph (1996), who investigate optimal emission taxation in an open economy.

29. If all firms reside in *one* region, say in region j, implying $E_{\tau j}^{-j} = Q_{\tau j}^{-j} = 0$, and if U_g equals unity, we would get Ebert's (1992) result (or Barnett's (1980) result if we deal with a monopoly). A generalization of this can be found in Requate (1994), who considers heterogeneous firms that are subject to uniform taxation.

30. Also, if the number of competing regions becomes large, the emission tax converges in the limit $(n \longrightarrow \infty)$ to the Pigouvian emission tax, if pollution is purely local.

31. Bold-faced off-diagonal entries indicate that all respective elements, above or under the diagonal, have the same value.

32. For the special case where the marginal values of public funds are equal to unity, there is no pollutant transmission, $\tilde{D}_e = -U_e^j$, and all firms reside in one jurisdiction, i.e., all firms face the same tax rates, $\tau^j = \bar{\tau} \, \forall j$, the tax rates derived here reduce to the formula given by Requate (1994) (cf. equation (3.6) therein).

33. Note that the sum of these effects may even be smaller than the single effect resulting from an increase of τ^j on the public revenue of region j, in general. Therefore, little can be said about whether the fiscal terms of the equilibrium tax rates, given by the second parts of (3.21), $((1-U_g^j)/U_g^j)(E^j/E_{\tau j}^j)$, fall short, equal, or exceed their cooperative counterparts, given by $J\vec{E}(\vec{\tau})'^{-1}(I_n - \tilde{U}_g)\vec{E}$ of equation (3.30). Only for the special case of two regions, does the comparison of the fiscal parts of the equilibrium and the second-best tax rates yield an unambiguous result. (See Proposition 3.6.)

34. This mitigates to some extent our inefficiency result of Proposition 3.3, for, roughly speaking, the deviation of the Nash tax rates from their Pigouvian levels exhibits the 'right sign', provided that first-best is not feasible.

35. In deriving (3.32), we have used the fact that the determinant of an $n \times n$

matrix of type

$$\begin{bmatrix} a & & b \\ & \ddots & \\ b & & a \end{bmatrix}$$

is given by $(a-b)^{n-1}(a+(n-1)b)$ and that adding up the elements of any row of the corresponding complementary matrix is equal to $(a-b)^{n-1}$.

36. Recall that trade does not emerge between identical regions, and, therefore, a terms-of-trade effect is neither present in the equilibrium, (3.25), nor in the optimal tax formula, (3.32).

4. Tax Competition, Provision of Public Goods, and Environmental Policy

1 INTRODUCTION

Within the last decade much work has been done in the theory of inter-jurisdictional tax competition. Zodrow and Mieszkowski (1986), Mintz and Tulkens (1986), Wilson (1986, 1987), and others showed that, under fairly general assumptions, interregional competition in tax rates on mobile capital leads to underprovision of local public goods. The extent of inefficiency depends – apart from the variety of policy tools (Bucovetsky and Wilson, 1991, and Hoyt, 1991a) – on the number of competing jurisdictions (Hoyt, 1991b), and on a thorough specification of the policy instruments if we deal with imperfect competition (Wildasin, 1988).

The establishment and imposition of environmental taxes, in particular emission taxes, that has been observed in recent years, influences capital flows through its impact on the net return to capital. Hence, the outcome of interjurisdictional competition and the provision of local public goods are determined by fiscal, industrial, and environmental policy. Therefore, a deliberate modelling of these aspects, including emission taxation and the behaviour of non-competitive firms, is indispensable. However, a general treatment of these political interrelations within a framework of limited policy tools (second-best analysis) is still missing. Because of this persistent gap between political significance and theoretical treatment, we integrate interjurisdictional tax competition and environmental policy in one model.[1]

Our model is structured as follows. Each local government maximizes the utility of some representative resident of its jurisdiction. To achieve this, it chooses two tax rates, one on capital and one on pollutant emissions, and the supply of two local public goods that benefit local industry and residents, respectively. The utility of the representative resident depends on the consumption of a private good, the prevailing environmental quality, and the provision of the residential public good. She receives income from her share of stocks of the local industry and from her capital endowment. The local firm produces an internationally (or interregionally) traded good by the use of capital and environmental inputs (pollutant emissions). On the output market the firm behaves non-competitively; namely, we assume that it has monopolistic power. (The analysis could also easily be adapted to the case of a small competitive firm.) By referring to the case of a small number of jurisdictions, we also consider non-competitive behaviour of the local governments. In this case, since the supply of national capital is assumed to be fixed, the local government has some non-negligible impact on the nation-wide net return to capital.

Although we introduce an additional policy tool, the emission tax rate, the inefficiency of the public sector perseveres, because local governments take a 'within viewpoint' and neglect pecuniary interjurisdictional externalities, namely the shift in tax bases.[2] Hence, interjurisdictional tax competition does not lead to efficiency, in general. However, the main result of the public finance literature dealing with interjurisdictional tax competition – underprovision of local public goods – is only half of the truth if we incorporate environmental policy.[3] Contrary to the well known result of unambiguous underprovision of public services, we find that overprovision may also occur. Whether under- or overprovision emerges depends crucially on the local initial capital endowment and on the influence of local policy on the equilibrium nation-wide net return to capital. For the special case of a small region, *two regimes* may occur: the first one is characterized by *underprovision of public goods*, a positive tax rate on capital, and *overprovision of environmental quality*; whereas the second one exhibits *overprovision of public goods*, a negative tax rate on capital, and *underprovision of environmental quality*.

This result may seem to be counterintuitive at first glance. Note, however, that if the local government has no (free) access to public funds through head taxation, local public goods must be financed either by capital or by emission taxation. Because capital is perfectly mobile, in equilibrium the tax rate on capital is too low from the efficiency point of view to prevent capital from flowing towards other regions. The emission tax, on the other hand, is too high, i.e., it exceeds marginal damage, since it not only serves to internalize the externality but also to finance public services. In the second regime, residents suffer to such a large extent from a deterioration of the environmental quality that the efficient emission tax is such that the induced tax revenue exceeds the cost of the first-best provision level of public services. Even the tax revenue collected from a lower emission tax implies, besides an inefficiently low environmental quality, overprovision of local public goods. Thus, if regions behave competitively (small regions), we have a striking new result: interjurisdictional tax competition either leads to underprovision of public goods and simultaneously to a too high environmental quality or we have overprovision of public services and a too low environmental quality.

While a Nash equilibrium is inefficient, in general, the question arises how a higher authority (e.g., a federal regulator) can influence the equilibrium allocation such that overall welfare is improved. If the central government is authorized to correct the outcome of interregional tax competition by applying a *non-revenue-neutral* interjurisdictional transfer schedule, namely to pay subsidies and penalties on local tax rates, efficiency can be re-established. More precisely, we demonstrate, for the case of a small region, that if in the first (second) regime capital taxation is subsidized (penalized) and emission taxation is penalized (subsidized) appropriately, public goods are provided efficiently and the emission tax equals the marginal environmental damage.[4]

If the federal authority is not authorized to apply regionally differentiated subsidy/penalty schemes, we cannot hope to reach a nation-wide Pareto improvement by either enhancing or lowering all tax rates symmetrically. Even in the special case of (quasi-)identical regions that differ only with respect to their initial capital endowments, a symmetric variation of the capital or emission tax rates, evaluated at a symmetric Nash equilibrium, does not imply a welfare improvement in every region. Only if all regions are perfectly identical (i.e., the initial endowments are the same everywhere), may such a policy measure lead to a Pareto improvement.

This chapter is structured as follows. In the next section we set up our model. Its basic ingredients are the local government, the residents, and the local industry. For the purpose of subsequent welfare analysis, we also depict the dependence of factor demand on the local policy tools. By means of this, in Section 3 we portray the optimal policy of one single local government, given the behaviour of its local industry and of all other governments. In particular, we refer to two special cases: a small region that cannot affect the nation-wide net return to capital and where one production factor is fixed on the short term. In Section 4 we consider possibilities of interference by the federal government which seeks to correct the equilibrium outcome of interjurisdictional tax competition. The last section summarizes the previous results.

2 THE MODEL

2.1 Local Governments

Consider a nation (or union) which is made up of n regions (or states), each of them consisting of identical residents. The (representative) residents of different jurisdictions need not be identical. Each local government is authorized to levy a specific tax on emissions, τ_e, as well as on capital, τ_k. The imposed tax system serves the twofold purpose of financing the provision of two local public goods and of affecting industrial pollutant emissions, E. The latter determine the environmental quality, U. We assume that U is a decreasing, concave function of pollutant emissions, $U = g(E)$, where $g' < 0$ and $g'' < 0$. Because no other tax instruments are available to the local government – in particular head taxes (lump sum transfers) are excluded – we are essentially concerned with second-best analysis.

Following Zodrow and Mieszkowski (1986), each local government provides two public goods: one that benefits residents and one that benefits industry.[5] To provide local public goods, the government uses a twofold one-to-one production technology. That is, the government is able to transform one unit of the private numéraire good into one unit of either the residential or the industrial public good.[6] Denote by P_i and P_r the provision level of the industrial and of the residential local public good, respectively. Then, the (local) public budget constraint, equating expenditure and tax revenue, is given by

$$P_i + P_r = \tau_k K + \tau_e E, \qquad (4.1)$$

where K and E represent the industrial use of capital and emissions. (As long as there is no room for doubt, we omit upper indices which would otherwise serve to indicate the region referred to.)

2.2 Residents

The welfare of the representative resident depends on the consumption of a private good, X, the prevailing environmental quality, U, and the supply of the residential local public good, P_r. Accordingly, her utility function can be written as

$$\mathcal{U}(X, U, P_r), \tag{4.2}$$

where $\mathcal{U}$ is strictly increasing and continuously differentiable in all its arguments. Residents take the environmental quality as well as the provision level of the local public good as given. Since they consume only one private good, they have no other choice than to spend their whole income on this item.

By neglecting the labour market, each resident's income is exclusively determined by non-labour income, which is the sum of her share, $\beta \in [0, 1]$, of the profit of the local firm,[7] Π, and of her portion, $\theta \in [0, 1]$, of the national capital stock, $\bar{K}$, times the nation-wide net return rate of capital, ρ. Hence, the private budget constraint is given by

$$X = \beta\Pi + \rho\theta\bar{K}, \tag{4.3}$$

where the consumption good serves as a numéraire. Note that while private income, the right hand side of (4.3), is, from the individual's viewpoint, exogenously given, a tax on profit or interest income would not distort consumers' behaviour trivially, but act as a head tax. Hence, since we want to focus on distortionary taxation, we exclude the possibility of profit or interest taxes.

2.3 Local Industry

In each jurisdiction there is a local firm producing some output good by the use of capital, K, and pollutant emissions, E. The production technology depends on the provision level of the local industrial public good, P_i (e.g., infrastructure), such that the firm's output can be written as $Q = F(K, E; P_i)$. The production function F is assumed to be strictly increasing and concave in all its variables.

Assume that the local firm represents a large exporting industry selling its output on an international market. This implies that the item produced and sold by the firm is different from that consumed by local residents. Thus, while the consumer good is produced either in some other region or abroad, local residents' welfare does not directly depend on the firm's output decisions.[8] Moreover, assume that the firm has monopolistic market power, facing a downward sloping inverse world demand curve, p, which is not 'too convex' in the sense that

$$p'' < -\frac{2p'}{Q} \quad \forall Q \in \mathbb{R}_+. \tag{4.4}$$

Condition (4.4) ensures that the revenue $\tilde{R}(Q) := p(Q)Q$ is strictly concave in Q which, together with the concavity of F, implies that revenue $R(K, E; P_i) := \tilde{R}(F(K, E; P_i))$ is also strictly concave in all its arguments.[9]

Let ρ denote the net price of capital; then, the after-tax price of capital is given by $p_k := \rho + \tau_k$, whereas the after-tax price of environmental inputs (emissions) equals its tax rate, $p_e := \tau_e$. Thus, the firm's profit is given by

$$\pi(K, E; p_k, p_e, P_i) = p(Q)F(K, E; P_i) - p_k K - p_e E, \tag{4.5}$$

where $Q = F(K, E; P_i)$. The firm maximizes, for any given p_k, p_e, and P_i, its profit with respect to K and E yielding the first-order conditions,

$$R_k = (p + p'Q)F_k = \rho + \tau_k, \tag{4.6}$$
$$R_e = (p + p'Q)F_e = \tau_e. \tag{4.7}$$

(Subindices of functions denote partial derivatives unless stated otherwise.) In conjunction with $Q = F(K, E; P_i)$, (4.6) and (4.7) implicitly define the (unconditional) factor demands for capital, $K(p_k, p_e, P_i)$, and emissions, $E(p_k, p_e, P_i)$. Substituting this into (4.5) gives the reduced profit function which depends on factor prices and the supply of industrial public services, exclusively:[10]

$$\Pi(p_k, \tau_e, P_i) := p\left(F(K(\cdot), E(\cdot); P_i)\right) F(K(\cdot), E(\cdot); P_i) - p_k K(\cdot) - \tau_e E(\cdot). \tag{4.8}$$

From now on, we denote by K, E, and Q the firm's *optimal* values of its production variables and by p the resulting *market clearing* price of its output, implicitly given by the firm's first-order conditions, the production function, and the the inverse demand curve, respectively.[11]

Suppose that, in the neighbourhood of the market equilibrium, F satisfies[12]

$$F_{ke} \leq -F_k F_e (2p' + p''Q)/(p + p'Q). \tag{4.9}$$

Condition (4.9) guarantees that the signs of the cross-price derivatives of factor demand, K_{p_e} and E_{p_k}, are unique, which will soon become clear.

2.4 Comparative Statics of Factor Demands

First, we investigate the firm's behaviour with respect to variations of the factor prices. To see how the firm reacts to a change of p_k and p_e, differentiate (4.6) and (4.7) totally for a fixed supply level of industrial public services, $P_i = \bar{P}_i$. This procedure yields, in matrix notation,

$$\begin{bmatrix} dK \\ dE \end{bmatrix} = \frac{1}{det(Hess(R))} \begin{bmatrix} R_{ee} & -R_{ke} \\ -R_{ke} & R_{kk} \end{bmatrix} \begin{bmatrix} dp_k \\ dp_e \end{bmatrix}, \tag{4.10}$$

where $det(Hess(R))$ denotes the determinant of the Hessian matrix of $R(K, E; \bar{P}_i)$. Due to the strict concavity of R, we know that $Hess(R)$ is negative definite and hence

$$R_{kk} < 0, \quad R_{ee} < 0, \quad det(Hess(R)) = R_{kk}R_{ee} - R_{ke}^2 > 0.$$

From (4.10) we get the partial derivatives of factor demand with respect to factor prices:[13]

$$K_{p_k} = \frac{R_{ee}}{det(Hess(R))}, \qquad K_{p_e} = -\frac{R_{ke}}{det(Hess(R))}, \tag{4.11}$$

$$E_{p_k} = -\frac{R_{ke}}{det(Hess(R))}, \qquad E_{p_e} = \frac{R_{kk}}{det(Hess(R))}. \tag{4.12}$$

To find out the signs of these derivatives, the following lemma provides a useful tool.

Lemma 4.1 R_{ke} *is non-positive.*

Proof: $R_{ke} \leq 0$ follows from (4.9) and (4.4). To see this, write R_{ke} explicitly as

$$R_{ke} = (2p' + Qp'')F_e F_k + (p + Qp')F_{ke},$$

which is clearly non-positive. □

If the number of regions is not too large, each government has, by means of its tax rate, some impact on the equilibrium net return rate of capital. For further analysis, we also need to know the signs of the derivatives of the net return to capital with respect to the local tax rates, $\partial \rho / \partial \tau_k^j$ and $\partial \rho / \partial \tau_e^j$.

Lemma 4.2 $-1 \leq \partial \rho / \partial \tau_k^j \leq 0$ *and* $\partial \rho / \partial \tau_e^j \geq 0$ $\forall j$.

Proof: Consider the market-clearing condition for capital,

$$\sum_{j=1}^{n} K^j (\underbrace{\rho(\cdot) + \tau_k^j}_{=p_k^j}, \tau_e^j, P_i^j) = \bar{K}, \tag{4.13}$$

where $\bar{K}$ denotes the fixed aggregate supply of capital. (4.13) implicitly defines the equilibrium net rate of capital as a function of *all* local tax rates and supply levels of public goods, $\rho\left(\tau_k^1, \ldots, \tau_k^n; \tau_e^1, \ldots, \tau_e^n; P_i^1, \ldots, P_i^n\right)$. Differentiating (4.13), for fixed provision levels of industrial public goods, with respect to τ_k^j yields

$$-1 \leq \frac{\partial \rho}{\partial \tau_k^j} = -\frac{K_{p_k^j}^j}{\sum_i K_{p_k^i}^i} \leq 0. \tag{4.14}$$

Analogously, differentiating (4.13) with respect to τ_e^j yields

$$\frac{\partial \rho}{\partial \tau_e^j} = -\frac{K_{\tau_e^j}^j}{\sum_i K_{p_k^i}^i} \geq 0. \tag{4.15}$$

Since we know from (4.11) and from Lemma 4.1 that the partial derivative K_{p_e} is non-negative, the derivative of ρ with respect to τ_e^j is also non-negative. This completes our proof.   □

Often, however, we may be interested in the dependence of the factor demand on tax rates rather than on factor prices. In particular, this may be the case if ρ is not constant but depends on the local tax rates. Using

$$dp_k = \left(1 + \frac{\partial \rho}{\partial \tau_k}\right) d\tau_k + \frac{\partial \rho}{\partial \tau_e} d\tau_e,$$

we can evaluate the total effects of the tax rates on factor demand by solving (4.10) for the desired derivatives:

$$\frac{\partial K}{\partial \tau_k} = \frac{R_{ee}}{\det(Hess(R))} \left(1 + \frac{\partial \rho}{\partial \tau_k}\right), \tag{4.16}$$

$$\frac{\partial K}{\partial \tau_e} = -\frac{R_{ke}}{det(Hess(R))}\left(1 - \frac{R_{ee}}{R_{ke}}\frac{\partial \rho}{\partial \tau_e}\right), \qquad (4.17)$$

$$\frac{\partial E}{\partial \tau_k} = -\frac{R_{ke}}{det(Hess(R))}\left(1 + \frac{\partial \rho}{\partial \tau_k}\right), \qquad (4.18)$$

$$\frac{\partial E}{\partial \tau_e} = \frac{R_{kk}}{det(Hess(R))}\left(1 - \frac{R_{ke}}{R_{kk}}\frac{\partial \rho}{\partial \tau_e}\right). \qquad (4.19)$$

Note that (4.11) and (4.12) already represent the total marginal changes of K and E if we deal with a small region which has no impact on the nation-wide net return to capital. In this case, we have $\partial K/\partial \tau_k|_{\rho=const.} = K_{p_k}$ and $\partial E/\partial \tau_k|_{\rho=const.} = E_{p_k}$, and similarly for the derivatives with respect to τ_e and p_e.

Using Lemma 4.2, we know from (4.16) and (4.18) that

$$\frac{\partial K}{\partial \tau_k} \le 0, \quad \text{and} \quad \frac{\partial E}{\partial \tau_k} \ge 0.$$

A rise of the tax rate on capital unambiguously induces a substitution of capital by environmental inputs. However, the same need not be true for the emission tax. Since a change of τ_e also affects the price of capital, the induced substitution effect is vague, in general; but, at least, for the special case of identical regions, we can determine the derivatives with respect to τ_e. Using

$$\frac{\partial \rho}{\partial \tau_k} = -\frac{1}{n} \quad \text{and} \quad \frac{\partial \rho}{\partial \tau_e} = -\frac{1}{n}\frac{K_{p_e}}{K_{p_k}},$$

(4.17) and (4.19) reduce to

$$\frac{\partial K}{\partial \tau_e} = -\frac{R_{ke}}{R_{kk}R_{ee} - R_{ke}^2}\frac{n-1}{n} > 0, \qquad (4.20)$$

$$\frac{\partial E}{\partial \tau_e} = \frac{1}{R_{ee}}\frac{R_{kk}R_{ee} - \frac{1}{n}R_{ke}^2}{R_{kk}R_{ee} - R_{ke}^2} \le \frac{1}{R_{ee}} < 0. \qquad (4.21)$$

In the case of identical regions, an increase of the price of environmental inputs unambiguously induces substitution of emissions by capital.

3 WELFARE ANALYSIS

In this section we investigate each region's optimal policy and the resulting equilibrium outcome of interjurisdictional tax competition.[14] Assume that, for any given behaviour of the other governments, each local government seeks to maximize the utility of its representative resident with respect to the (locally) available policy instruments. We can think of local governments autonomously, i.e., non-cooperatively, solving constrained optimization problems, the solutions of which define the regions' reaction curves. Since at a Nash equilibrium no local government has an incentive to deviate unilaterally from its equilibrium strategy, its policy must be optimal in the sense that it cannot improve its resident's welfare by altering any policy variable. In other words, the system of the reaction curves implicitly defines, as a fixed point, the vector of equilibrium variables – the Nash tax rates and provision levels of interjurisdictional tax competition.

Since the number of competing regions is relatively small, each government recognizes that it has some impact on the capital market. That is, each government takes into account the change of the allocation of capital and of the equilibrium net return to capital resulting from its (local) policy. In addition, we also refer to the case of a small region which has no influence on national prices and views ρ as exogenously given.

3.1 Equilibrium Policy of a Local Government

By means of the previous analysis, we know the dependence of capital demand and of the net return to capital on the capital tax rates. This enables us to solve the (parametric) optimization problem of a local regulator, given that she maximizes the utility of her representative resident subject to the private (4.3) and the public budget constraint (4.1) with respect to her policy tools – the tax rates on capital and pollutant emissions and the provision levels of the residential and the industrial local public good – taking any behaviour of the other governments as given. Substituting (4.3) into (4.2) and differentiating the Lagrangian with respect to τ_k, τ_e, P_i, and P_r yields

$$
\begin{aligned}
\frac{\partial \mathcal{L}}{\partial \tau_k} &= \lambda \left[E_{p_k}(1+\rho_{\tau_k})\tau_e + K_{p_k}(1+\rho_{\tau_k})\tau_k + K \right] \\
&\quad + \mathcal{U}_x \left(\beta \Pi_{p_k}(1+\rho_{\tau_k}) + \bar{K}\theta\rho_{\tau_k} \right) \\
&\quad + \mathcal{U}_u g' E_{p_k}(1+\rho_{\tau_k}) = 0, \quad\quad\quad (4.22)
\end{aligned}
$$

$$
\frac{\partial \mathcal{L}}{\partial \tau_e} = \lambda \left[\tau_e (E_{p_e} + E_{p_k}\rho_{\tau_e}) + \tau_k (K_{p_e} + K_{p_k}\rho_{\tau_e}) + E \right]
$$

$$+ U_x \left(\beta(\Pi_{p_e} + \Pi_{p_k}\rho_{\tau_e}) + \bar{K}\theta\rho_{\tau_e} \right)$$
$$+ U_u g' \left(E_{p_e} + E_{p_k}\rho_{\tau_e} \right) = 0, \tag{4.23}$$

$$\frac{\partial \mathcal{L}}{\partial P_i} = \lambda \left[-1 + \tau_e(E_{P_i} + E_{p_k}\rho_{P_i}) + \tau_k(K_{P_i} + K_{p_k}\rho_{P_i}) \right]$$
$$+ U_x \left(\beta(\Pi_{P_i} + \Pi_{p_k}\rho_{P_i}) + \bar{K}\theta\rho_{P_i} \right)$$
$$+ U_u g' \left(E_{P_i} + E_{p_k}\rho_{P_i} \right) = 0, \tag{4.24}$$

$$\frac{\partial \mathcal{L}}{\partial P_r} = -\lambda + U_{P_r} = 0, \tag{4.25}$$

where λ is the Lagrangian multiplier of the public budget constraint. Note that the terms in square brackets within these equations represent the marginal public revenue stemming from a rise of τ_k, τ_e, and P_i, respectively. Then, λ times the term in square brackets of (4.24) equals the social marginal cost of providing an additional unit of the industrial public good, whereas the social price of the residential public good equals λ.

From the firm's optimization conditions we know by the envelope theorem that $\Pi_{p_k} = -K$, $\Pi_{p_e} = -E$, and that $\Pi_{P_i} = (p + p'Q)F_{P_i}$. Substituting this into (4.22), (4.23), and (4.24), we can derive the marginal rates of substitution between the private good and the residential public good, on the one hand, and between the private good and environmental quality, on the other hand. Beyond this, we also 'solve' the first-order conditions for the tax rates, τ_k and τ_e. With regard to the industrial public good, we infer the marginal rate of transformation between the private and industrial public good.

Solving (4.22), (4.23), and (4.24) for the marginal rates of substitution of the private good for environmental quality respectively for the public good, we get

$$\frac{U_u}{U_x} = -\frac{1}{g'} \left[-\beta \left(E\frac{\partial P_r}{\partial \tau_k} - K\frac{\partial P_r}{\partial \tau_e} \right) + (\beta K - \theta\bar{K}) \left(-\rho_{\tau_e}\frac{\partial P_r}{\partial \tau_k} + \rho_{\tau_k}\frac{\partial P_r}{\partial \tau_e} \right) \right]$$
$$\div \left[\left(E_{p_e}\frac{\partial P_r}{\partial \tau_k} - E_{p_k}\frac{\partial P_r}{\partial \tau_e} \right) - E_{p_k} \left(-\rho_{\tau_e}\frac{\partial P_r}{\partial \tau_k} + \rho_{\tau_k}\frac{\partial P_r}{\partial \tau_e} \right) \right] \tag{4.26}$$

$$\frac{U_{P_r}}{U_x} = \beta \left[(1+\rho_{\tau_k}) - (1+\rho_{\tau_k})\frac{EE_{p_k}}{KE_{p_e}} + \left(\rho_{\tau_e}\frac{E_{p_k}}{E_{p_e}} - \rho_{\tau_k} \right)\frac{\theta\bar{K}}{\beta K} \right]$$
$$\div \left[1 + (1+\rho_{\tau_k})\tau_k\frac{K_{p_k}}{K} - \frac{E_{p_k}}{E_{p_e}} \left[(1+\rho_{\tau_k}) \left(\frac{E}{K} + \tau_k\frac{K_{p_e}}{K} \right) - \rho_{\tau_e} \right] \right] \tag{4.27}$$

$$= \beta \left[1 - (1+\rho_{\tau_k}) \frac{E E_{p_k}}{K E_{p_e}} + \rho_{\tau_e} \frac{E_{p_k}}{E_{p_e}} \frac{\theta \bar{K}}{\beta K} + \rho_{\tau_k} \frac{\beta K - \theta \bar{K}}{\beta K} \right] \qquad (4.28)$$

$$\div \left[1 - (1+\rho_{\tau_k}) \frac{E E_{p_k}}{K E_{p_e}} + \rho_{\tau_e} \frac{E_{p_k}}{E_{p_e}} + \frac{\tau_k (1+\rho_{\tau_k})}{K E_{p_e}} [K_{p_k} E_{p_e} - E_{p_k} K_{p_e}] \right].$$

While these expressions depend on, among other things, the interregional distribution of capital income and the influence of the policy instruments on the nation-wide net return to capital, they look a bit unwieldy. However, this very general approach of interjurisdictional tax competition exhibits some important features which do not appear simultaneously in simpler ones, if ever. In order to show how this model is related to other, less general, models we simplify our approach below. But first of all, we give some interpretations of our general approach, i.e., of (4.26) and (4.27) (or (4.28)).

Both marginal rates of substitution depend on the steepness of the Laffer curves, $\partial P_r / \partial \tau_k$ and $\partial P_r / \partial \tau_e$, on the elasticities of local factor demand, on the sensitivities of the net return to capital, ρ_{τ_k} and ρ_{τ_e}, and on the (effective) local excess demand of capital, $\beta K - \theta \bar{K}$. The term $\rho_{\tau_k} (\beta K - \theta \bar{K})/(\beta K)$ represents the cost change of the (effective) net capital import per unit resulting from a rise of τ_k. Note that, as long as $\beta < 1$, local consumers do not bear the full costs of industrial capital demand. The effective capital cost *perceived* by local residents equals $\rho \beta$ and is therefore lower than the social cost of capital, ρ.

Consider the marginal rate of substitution of the private for the public good, given in (4.28). The second term of the numerator as well as of the denominator, $(E_{p_k}/E_{p_e})(E/K)(1+\rho_{\tau_k})$, reflects the fact that raising an additional unit of public funds has an indirect effect on pollutant emissions by altering the industrial input ratios due to factor substitution. As we already know, $1 + \rho_{\tau_k}$ is positive, i.e., a rise of the tax rate on capital increases its consumer price and therefore induces a substitution of capital by emissions. Hence, raising τ_k implies indirect negative welfare effects by means of a lower environmental quality. This effect increases the (social) price of local public goods; in addition, the same effect also distorts the tax basis similarly. Therefore, the same term is also present in the denominator, and if no other effects occurred, the marginal rate of substitution between the private and the public good would be equal to β. For the special case, where β is equal to one, the effective marginal cost of public services coincides with its social (i.e., national) marginal cost, because local residents bear the full provision costs.[15]

Yet, there are further effects present that prevent the local government from providing public services efficiently. The third and the fourth term of the numerator as well as of the denominator of (4.28) cause the marginal rate of substitution between the private and the public good to differ from the marginal rate of transformation, which is equal to unity. This remains true even if we consider the special case of $\beta = 1$. First, if we inspect the respective third parts, we see that the numerator declines more than the denominator if $\theta \bar{K} / \beta K > 1$. In this case, the provision of the public good becomes less expensive. For a net-capital-exporting region, the rise of the net return to capital resulting from an increase of τ_e is partially borne by non-residents. Because the net return has to some extent to be paid by non-residents, the consumers of capital-exporting regions benefit from an increase of ρ: they succeed in shifting some portion of the provision cost of their public goods to residents of capital-importing regions. (The opposite is true for net-capital-importing regions.)

The interpretation of the fourth part of the numerator is completely analogous, except that we are concerned with an increase of the capital rather than of the emission tax. Since ρ depends negatively on τ_k, the provision of public goods becomes less expensive for capital-importing regions; but more expensive for capital-exporting regions. Thus, *ceteris paribus*, capital-exporting regions favour emission taxation, whereas capital-importing regions prefer capital taxation in order to raise public funds.

As already indicated, the second main effect – besides the 'terms-of-trade effect' resulting from excess supply (or demand) of capital – is responsible for the inefficient provision of public goods stemming from distortionary taxation. Among other things, the fourth term of the denominator reflects how capital and emission taxation affect their own tax bases. At a first glance, the sign of the fourth term of the denominator seems to be ambiguous. However, while E_{p_e} is negative by (4.12) and we have $0 \leq 1 + \rho_{\tau_k} \leq 1$ by (4.14), the sign of the fourth term just depends on $K_{p_k} E_{p_e} - E_{p_k} K_{p_e}$. But this term equals the inverse of the determinant of the Hessian matrix of the revenue, $1/(R_{kk} R_{ee} - R_{ke}^2)$, which is positive since R is strictly concave.[16] Hence, the denominator of (4.28) is smaller than $1 - (1 + \rho_{\tau_k})(E_{p_k}/E_{p_e})(E/K)$ if τ_k is positive.[17]

The numerator, however, *may* become larger than this expression by the last two terms, even for positive tax rates. This enables us to derive a necessary and sufficient condition for under- and overprovision of public goods. Let $\varepsilon_{p_k}^k := p_k K_{p_k}/K$ denote the (own-price) elasticity of capital demand.

Proposition 4.1 *If local residents hold all stocks of the local firm, $\beta = 1$, over-(under)provision of local public goods occurs if, and only if, initial capital endowment satisfies*

$$\frac{\theta \bar{K}}{K} \underset{(>)}{<} 1 - \varepsilon_{p_k}^k \frac{\tau_k}{\rho + \tau_k} \frac{1 + \rho_{\tau_k}}{\rho_{\tau_k}}. \qquad (4.29)$$

Clearly if the right hand side of (4.29) is negative, overprovision of public goods does not emerge, regardless of the initial capital endowment. Provided that the tax rate on capital is positive, overprovision of local public goods can only occur in capital-importing regions, i.e., we have underprovision in all exporting regions. However, the right hand side may not only be positive, but even be larger than one if τ_k is negative. In this case, overprovision of public goods can only occur in capital-exporting regions, whereas public goods are overprovided in importing regions. If the elasticity of capital demand is equal to zero, local public goods are over-(under)provided if, and only if, $\theta \bar{K}/K < 1(> 1)$. Each net-capital-importing (exporting) jurisdiction overprovides (underprovides) local public services.

Roughly speaking, Proposition 4.1 states that overprovision is the more likely the lower the (relative) initial capital endowment. The intuition behind this is the following. Those regions which are well endowed with capital suffer extra costs from capital taxation by inducing a decrease of the net return to capital. The contrary is true for regions poorly endowed with capital. Because their residents hold a relatively small portion of the national capital stock, the decline of the net return to capital resulting from an increase of the local capital tax rate does not bother them much. In this sense, the decline of the net return to capital acts as a subsidy for those regions which are poorly endowed with capital. If this effect is sufficiently strong, the local government tends to raise the tax rate on capital to such a large extent that the tax revenue may 'skyrocket' beyond the point of efficient provision of local public goods and thus overprovision occurs. The contrary is true for regions relatively well endowed with capital. Since they hesitate to tighten the tax screw on capital, they rely more heavily on emission taxation. Therefore, over-provision of public services is 'less likely' for capital-exporting regions, and may only emerge if $\tau_k < 0$.

This result shows that we cannot rule out overprovision of local public goods, in general. In particular, if the regional distribution of capital is sufficiently unequal (measured in excess demand/supply), overprovision may emerge in those regions most poorly endowed with capital. For the special case where in each region the excess demand of capital equals zero, $\theta \bar{K} = K$, we have the following corollary of Proposition 4.1.

Corollary 4.1 *If capital demand exactly equals local initial capital endowment, over-(under)provision of local public goods occurs if, and only if, capital is taxed at a negative (positive) rate.*

To get some intuition of this result, fix, for a moment, the emission tax at its Pigouvian level, i.e., at the social marginal damage of pollutant emission, and assume that the tax rate on capital is zero. Then, one of two cases occurs: the public revenue resulting from emission taxation either exceeds or falls short of the public revenue which would be necessary to provide public services efficiently. If the emission tax raises too much public funds, the government redistributes some revenue to consumers through a subsidy on capital; in the other case, it raises additional revenue by imposing a positive tax rate on capital.

Previous analysis suggests that underprovision is increasing in initial capital endowment, i.e., the marginal rate of substitution between the private and the public good, MRS_{xp}, is a monotonously increasing function of $\theta \bar{K}$. To prove this presumption, differentiate MRS_{xp} with respect to $\theta \bar{K}$, yielding

$$\frac{\partial \text{MRS}_{xp}}{\partial \theta \bar{K}} = -\frac{1}{\mathcal{N}} \frac{\rho_{T_k}}{K} \left(1 - \frac{\rho_{T_e}}{\rho_{T_k}} \frac{E_{p_k}}{E_{p_e}} \right) > 0, \qquad (4.30)$$

where $\mathcal{N} > 0$ denotes the denominator of (4.27) and (4.28). This gives us the following proposition, which is closely related to Proposition 4.1.

Proposition 4.2 *The marginal rate of substitution between the private and the public good is monotonously increasing in local initial capital endowment, $\theta \bar{K}$.*

This proposition confirms our previous result that the larger (smaller) the local capital endowment is, the more, *ceteris paribus*, local public goods are underprovided (overprovided).

Solving (4.22) and (4.23) for τ_k and τ_e, while using (4.25), gives[18]

$$\tau_k = \frac{(U_{P_r} - \beta U_x)(EE_{p_k} - KE_{p_e})}{U_{P_r}(E_{p_e}K_{p_k} - E_{p_k}K_{p_e})}$$
$$+ \frac{(U_{P_r}K - U_x\theta\bar{K})(E_{p_e}\rho_{\tau_k} - E_{p_k}\rho_{\tau_e})}{U_{P_r}(1 + \rho_{\tau_k})(E_{p_e}K_{p_k} - E_{p_k}K_{p_e})}, \tag{4.31}$$

$$\tau_e = -\frac{U_u g'}{U_{P_r}} + \frac{(U_{P_r} - \beta U_x)(KK_{p_e} - EK_{p_k})}{U_{P_r}(E_{p_e}K_{p_k} - E_{p_k}K_{p_e})}. \tag{4.32}$$

The tax rate on capital is composed of two parts. The first part results from distortionary taxation of industrial inputs, reflecting the extent of inefficient provision of local public goods, $(U_{P_r} - \beta U_x)$. The second part stems from the strategic effect provoked by an unequal distribution of capital. This effect is the larger, the more local capital demand exceeds its supply, $(U_{P_r}K - U_x\theta\bar{K})$. The sign of τ_k depends on these first two terms within each numerator because all other terms are positive. Recall that the sign of τ_k plays a crucial role, as already indicated in Proposition 4.1. Moreover, it is easy to show that τ_k depends negatively on $\theta\bar{K}$,

$$\frac{\partial \tau_k}{\partial \theta\bar{K}} = \frac{-U_x E_{p_e}\rho_{\tau_k}\left(1 - \frac{E_{p_k}}{E_{p_e}}\frac{\rho_{\tau_e}}{\rho_{\tau_k}}\right)}{U_{P_r}(1 + \rho_{\tau_k})(E_{p_e}K_{p_k} - E_{p_k}K_{p_e})} < 0. \tag{4.33}$$

Proposition 4.3 *The larger the local initial capital endowment, the lower,* ceteris paribus, *the local tax rate on capital.*

Proposition 4.3 emphasizes our previous finding that those regions which are relatively well endowed with capital tend, *ceteris paribus*, to tax capital less heavily than regions poorly endowed with capital. The intuition behind this should be clear from our preceding elucidation.

The emission tax, on the other hand, is made up of the marginal environmental damage resulting from pollutant emissions and a component stemming from distortionary taxation, which corresponds to the first term of the capital tax rate. While the marginal damage is clearly positive, the sign of the emission tax rate depends on the extent of under- (over)provision of public goods, $(U_{P_r} - \beta U_x)$. This gives us the following result.

Proposition 4.4 *If local residents hold all stocks of the local firm, $\beta =$ 1, the local government fixes the emission tax rate below (above) marginal social damage if, and only if, local public goods are over-(under)provided.*

The intuition behind this follows the line of argument given in the context of Proposition 4.1 and Corollary 4.1. Starting at the Pigouvian level of τ_e and fixing τ_k at zero, two cases may emerge: public revenue stemming from emission taxation either falls short or exceeds that level of public funds which is required to provide public services efficiently. If the revenue is too high (overprovision), the government seeks to mitigate this inefficiency by lowering the emission tax. Since this means a too low environmental quality, there is a trade-off between efficient provision of public goods and the optimal environmental quality. (The arguments are reversed if the revenue from efficient emission taxation implies underprovision of public services.)

From (4.32) we see that τ_e is independent of (i.e., not directly dependent on) the distribution of capital. The initial capital endowment does not, *ceteris paribus*, affect the emission tax rate, $\partial \tau_e / \partial \theta \bar{K} = 0$. Consequently, we do not get a similar result for the emission tax as we have derived for the capital tax rate (Proposition 4.3), but the following.

Proposition 4.5 *The local emission tax rate is, ceteris paribus, independent of the local initial capital endowment.*

A higher initial capital endowment leaves, *ceteris paribus*, τ_e unaffected, but lowers τ_k. So there is no (direct) substitution of capital taxation by emission taxation as the initial capital endowment increases. Yet, the link between both tax rates arises from the *endogenous* provision level of public goods (the distortionary taxation term).

Thus far we have neglected the provision of the industrial local public good. Since the supply level of the residential public good is inefficient, there are good reasons to presume that the industrial public good is also provided inefficiently. We inspect the effects that prompt the local governments to under- or oversupply industrial public services, by deriving the marginal rate of transformation between the private and the industrial public good. To achieve this, totally differentiate the private budget constraint for a fixed provision level of the residential public good. Using

$$d\rho = \frac{\partial \rho}{\partial \tau_k} d\tau_k + \frac{\partial \rho}{\partial \tau_e} d\tau_e + \frac{\partial \rho}{\partial P_i} dP_i,$$

this procedure yields

$$dX = \left(-\beta K + (\theta\bar{K}-\beta K)\frac{\partial\rho}{\partial\tau_k}\right)d\tau_k + \left(-\beta E + (\theta\bar{K}-\beta K)\frac{\partial\rho}{\partial\tau_e}\right)d\tau_e$$
$$+ \left(-\beta F_{P_i}(p+p'Q) + (\theta\bar{K}-\beta K)\frac{\partial\rho}{\partial P_i}\right)dP_i. \tag{4.34}$$

Analogously, totally differentiating the public budget constraint with $dP_r = 0$ and solving for dP_i yields

$$dP_i = \frac{\left[K+\tau_k K_{p_k}\left(1+\frac{\partial\rho}{\partial\tau_k}\right)\right]d\tau_k + \left[\tau_k K_{p_e}+\tau_k K_{p_k}\frac{\partial\rho}{\partial\tau_e}\right]d\tau_e}{1 - \tau_k\left(K_{P_i}+K_{p_k}\frac{\partial\rho}{\partial P_i}\right) - \tau_e\left(E_{P_i}+E_{p_k}\frac{\partial\rho}{\partial P_i}\right)}. \tag{4.35}$$

Setting $d\tau_e = 0$, substituting (4.35) into (4.34), and dividing both equations gives the marginal rate of transformation,[19]

$$-\frac{dX}{dP_i} = \frac{\beta K - (\theta\bar{K}-\beta K)\frac{\partial\rho}{\partial\tau_k}}{K+\tau_k K_{p_k}\left(1+\frac{\partial\rho}{\partial\tau_k}\right)+\tau_e E_{p_k}\left(1+\frac{\partial\rho}{\partial\tau_k}\right)}$$
$$\times\left[1-\tau_k\left(K_{P_i}+K_{p_k}\frac{\partial\rho}{\partial P_i}\right)-\tau_e\left(E_{P_i}+E_{p_k}\frac{\partial\rho}{\partial P_i}\right)\right]$$
$$-\beta F_{P_i}(p+p'Q)-(\theta\bar{K}-\beta K)\frac{\partial\rho}{\partial P_i}. \tag{4.36}$$

First, note that the (locally perceived) provision costs of industrial services consist of three parts: one direct and two indirect. The first part accounts for those units of private goods that have to be sacrificed to raise public revenue sufficiently to provide one additional unit of the industrial public good. The numerator represents the marginal impact of τ_k on private consumption whereas the denominator represents the marginal impact of τ_k on public revenue. Thus, we may interpret this fraction as the marginal rate of transformation between private income and public funds. Roughly speaking, this is the social marginal value of income, using governmental income as numéraire. Since the bracket term (second line of the right hand side of (4.36)) measures the marginal costs of industrial public services, the first added term represents the social value of the provision costs of one additional unit of the industrial public good.

In addition, there are two further factors that do not affect the public budget constraint. Because we deal with the provision of an *industrial* public good, enhancing the supply level of public services improves the production technology and therefore increases the profit of the local firm by $F_{P_i}(p + p'Q)$. Due to induced factor substitution, this in turn affects the equilibrium net return to capital and thereby the yield of local capital owners by $(\theta \bar{K} - \beta K)\frac{\partial \rho}{\partial P_i}$. Since local residents do not benefit directly from the provision of industrial public services, these two effects lowering the social provision costs already represent the total local gain accruing from the industrial public good. These benefits are redistributed to local residents by means of dividend and interest payments.

The optimal provision level of the industrial local public good is determined implicitly by equating the marginal rate of transformation between private income and public funds (direct marginal provision cost) and the social marginal benefits from the industrial public good (indirect benefits that accrue to local residents). Note that if local capital supply exactly meets local capital demand $(K = \theta \bar{K})$, if the local firm belongs entirely to local residents $(\beta = 1)$, and if there is no distortionary taxation, the direct costs are equal to unity.

To sum up, since industrial public services are not provided at that level where its marginal product is equal to its marginal cost, $pF_{P_i} = 1$, they are provided inefficiently. This is due to four effects: firstly, the distributive effect resulting from the fact that the region imports or exports capital; secondly, local residents do not own the local firm entirely; thirdly, the local firm does not act competitively; and fourthly, we are dealing with distortionary taxation.

3.2 The Special Case of a Small Region

Thus far we have seen that taxation of productive factors leads, through its impact on the net return to capital, to income shifts. Hence, fiscal and environmental policy have distributive effects. To remove this topic from our analysis for the moment, consider the special case of a small region which has no influence on national variables, especially on the nationwide net return to capital.[20] The government of a small region takes ρ as exogenously given, and its first-order conditions no longer (directly) depend on the local excess demand of capital. To see this, imagine a small jurisdiction where the residents hold all stocks of the local firm, i.e., $\beta = 1$. In this case, our above stated conditions (4.26), (4.27), and

(4.36) reduce to

$$-\frac{dX}{dU} = -\frac{-\frac{E}{K}\frac{\partial P_r}{\partial \tau_k} + \frac{\partial P_r}{\partial \tau_e}}{\frac{E_{p_e}}{K}\frac{\partial P_r}{\partial \tau_k} - \frac{E_{p_k}}{K}\frac{\partial P_r}{\partial \tau_e}}\frac{1}{g'} = \frac{1 - \frac{E}{K}\left(-\frac{d\tau_e}{d\tau_k}\right)}{\frac{E_{p_k}}{K} - \frac{E_{p_e}}{K}\left(-\frac{d\tau_e}{d\tau_k}\right)}\frac{1}{g'} \quad (4.37)$$

$$-\frac{dX}{dP_r} = \frac{1 - \left[\frac{E_{p_k}}{E_{p_e}}\frac{E}{K}\right]}{1 + \tau_k\frac{K_{p_k}}{K} - \left[\frac{E_{p_k}}{E_{p_e}}\left(\frac{E}{K} + \tau_k\frac{K_{p_e}}{K}\right)\right]}, \quad (4.38)$$

$$-\frac{dX}{dP_i} = \frac{K\left(1 - \tau_k K_{P_i} - \tau_e E_{P_i}\right)}{K + \tau_k K_{p_k} + \tau_e E_{p_k}} - F_{P_i}(p + p'Q), \quad (4.39)$$

where $-d\tau_e/d\tau_k$ denotes the marginal rate of technical (or fiscal) substitution between the two tax rates; it indicates at which rate the government has to increase one tax rate if the other is reduced and public revenue is kept constant. Observe that in conditions (4.37), (4.38), and (4.39) the local initial capital endowment no longer appears, i.e., distributional differences are erased. The assumption of β being equal to one implies that the region's residents bear the full operating cost of the firm. In this case, the local government has no incentive to tax away the profit of the firm; since there is no outflow of dividends, no welfare effects are induced by profit taxation and redistributing the revenue to residents.

If we rearrange (4.38), we see that the marginal rate of substitution between the private and the residential public good exceeds unity if, and only if, τ_k is positive. This means that *over*provision of local public goods does not occur if capital is taxed by positive amounts. To see this, rewrite (4.38) as

$$-\frac{dX}{dP_r} = \frac{1 - \frac{E}{K}\frac{E_{p_k}}{E_{p_e}}}{1 - \frac{E}{K}\frac{E_{p_k}}{E_{p_e}} + [E_{p_e}K_{p_k} - E_{p_k}K_{p_e}]\frac{\tau_k}{E_{p_e}K}}. \quad (4.40)$$

As we already know from our former analysis, the bracket term of the denominator is positive, which implies for $\tau_k > 0$ that the denominator is smaller than the numerator, meaning that the marginal rate of substitution is larger than one. Hence, contrary to our more general model where the net return to capital is endogenous, we can exclude the possibility of overprovision of local public goods if $\tau_k > 0$. (The contrary is true for $\tau_k < 0$.)

Proposition 4.6 *If a jurisdiction is sufficiently small, such that the nation-wide net return to capital is independent of the local tax rates, and residents hold all stocks of the local firm, $\beta = 1$, interjurisdictional tax competition leads to under-(over)provision of local public goods if, and only if, the tax rate on capital is positive (negative).*

Note that Proposition 4.6 gives us the same consequence as Corollary 4.1 which was derived for the special case where $\theta \bar{K} = K$. Hence, there is the same equivalence between the inefficiency of the public sector and capital taxation under the local market-clearing condition for capital as under the assumption of a small region.

For a further inspection, 'solve' (4.37) and (4.38), which define each region's equilibrium policy, for both tax rates. (Equivalently, evaluate (4.31) and (4.32) at $\beta = 1$ and when ρ is a given constant.)

$$\tau_k = \frac{(U_{P_r} - U_x)(EE_{p_k} - KE_{p_e})}{U_{P_r}(E_{p_e}K_{p_k} - E_{p_k}K_{p_e})} \tag{4.41}$$

$$\tau_e = -\frac{U_u g'}{U_{P_r}} + \frac{(U_{P_r} - U_x)(KK_{p_e} - EK_{p_k})}{U_{P_r}(E_{p_e}K_{p_k} - E_{p_k}K_{p_e})} \tag{4.42}$$

Contrary to our former, more general model, the signs of τ_k and of τ_e depend solely on the extent of inefficient provision of public goods, $U_{P_r} - U_x$. Since Proposition 4.4 particularly holds for the special case of a small region, we can compose Propositions 4.4 and 4.6. It follows that only two possible regimes may emerge:

Regime 1: *Under*provision of local public goods $\Leftrightarrow \tau_k > 0 \Leftrightarrow \tau_e > -U_u g'/U_{P_r}$.

Regime 2: *Over*provision of local public goods $\Leftrightarrow \tau_k < 0 \Leftrightarrow \tau_e < -U_u g'/U_{P_r}$.

This is a clear-cut, and possibly surprising, result: either the emission tax exceeds marginal social damage, implying '*over*provision' of environmental quality(!), or the emission tax is too low and we have '*under*provision' of environmental quality. In the first case (Regime 1), capital is taxed on a positive rate and public services are underprovided; while in the second case (Regime 2), capital is subsidized and public services are overprovided(!).

Since the local government is by no means able to influence the nation-wide net rate of capital, there are no strategic factors that affect the equilibrium values of the policy tools. The only distortionary effect that is still present results from non-neutral taxation. While the government seeks to raise public funds through capital and emission taxation, it distorts the production decisions of the industry. The second effect results from the externality that is caused by pollutant emissions.[21]

In the first-best case, where the local government is authorized to finance any desired level of public goods through head taxation, the optimal head tax is determined implicitly by $\partial \mathcal{U}/\partial P_r = \partial \mathcal{U}/\partial X$. The marginal rate of substitution between the (residential) public good and the private good would be equal to the marginal rate of transformation, which in turn is equal to unity. In a second-best world, however, this may emerge only by chance, if the revenue collected from the second-best emission tax rate exactly meets the expenditure required for the optimal provision level of local public goods. In this case, no further revenue is needed from capital taxation, and the local government leaves capital untaxed. We can see this from (4.37) by using the optimal tax rate on capital, $\tau_k = 0$, and solving for τ_e:

$$\tau_e = -\frac{\mathcal{U}_u g'}{\mathcal{U}_x} \geq 0. \tag{4.43}$$

In the social optimum, the emission tax rate is equal to the marginal willingness of the residents to pay for a better environment, i.e., the marginal damage.[22]

However, if the yield form the first-best tax rates, (4.43) and $\tau_k = 0$, falls short of the revenue required to provide public services efficiently, the government will raise additional funds through tightening the tax screw. This is done by increasing the emission beyond the Pigouvian level *and* by levying a positive tax rate on capital. Of course, this mitigates the extent of underprovision of public services; yet, the government hesitates to tax production factors more severely such that it could provide public goods efficiently. The reason is that the government is restricted to using distortionary taxes, i.e., taxes that evade their own bases. Thus, we have simultaneously a positive tax rate on capital, underprovision of public goods, and a too high environmental quality (Regime 1). Similar arguments illustrate that if the revenue raised through the first-best tax rates is too low to provide public services efficiently, we have: subsidization of capital, overprovision of public goods, and a too low environmental quality (Regime 2).

3.3 Short-Run Analysis

Thus far we have assumed that firms can respond to a change of tax rates by adjusting their factor demands appropriately. However, this may be unrealistic if, due to the installation of long-term durable investment goods, industrial capital is be fixed in the short run. Tax rates, however, can often be altered on short or at least on medium terms. Whenever an unexpected variation of the tax rates emerges, industry is urged to adjust non-capital factors exclusively if capital is fixed by long-term investments. This gives us reason to consider a model where industrial capital is fixed and the firm is only able to respond to changes of factor prices by adjusting its pollutant emissions. We assume, as before, that the firm takes the supply of industrial local public goods as well as the tax rates as given. Under these circumstances, an unexpected increase of τ_k does not affect the use of capital. But if K remains constant, the marginal product of pollutant emissions does not change either, implying that E also remains constant. The only derivative of factor demand that differs from zero is $\partial E/\partial \tau_e = 1/R_{ee} < 0$. Clearly, the capital market is not in equilibrium after the change of the tax rates, in general; and hence, ρ is not well defined by (4.13); nor are $\partial \rho/\partial \tau_k$ and $\partial \rho/\partial \tau_e$. To avoid any technical problems, assume that by long-term rent contracts the net return to capital is fixed for the whole investment period. Then, ρ is independent of local tax rates, $\partial \rho/\partial \tau_k = 0$, $\partial \rho/\partial \tau_e = 0$, and $\partial \rho/\partial P_i = 0$.[23] Using the modified first-order conditions

$$-\mathcal{U}_x \beta K + \mathcal{U}_{P_r} K = 0, \qquad (4.44)$$

$$-\mathcal{U}_x \beta E + \mathcal{U}_u g' E_{p_e} + \mathcal{U}_{P_r} (\tau_e E_{p_e} + E) = 0, \qquad (4.45)$$

$$\mathcal{U}_x \beta \Pi_{P_i} + \mathcal{U}_u g' E_{P_i} + \mathcal{U}_{P_r} (-1 + \tau_e E_{P_i}) = 0, \qquad (4.46)$$

it becomes clear that τ_k is adjusted in a way that the marginal rate of substitution between the private and the (residential) public good, $\mathcal{U}_{P_r}/\mathcal{U}_x$, is equal to its perceived marginal cost, β. The inelasticity of capital demand means that any distortionary effect of raising public funds is avoided; rather capital taxation serves the sole purpose of financing public goods. In other words, any desired level of public funds can be raised without affecting production in a distortionary manner. On the other hand, for $\beta = 1$ equation (4.45) implies, by using (4.44), that the emission tax rate is set according to its first-best formula, (4.43).

Consequently, if capital is demanded inelastically, the local government adjusts the emission tax rate at its first-best, i.e., the Pigouvian, level; whereas the capital tax rate is non-distortionary and acts as a lump sum tax to raise the efficient amount of public funds.

Proposition 4.7 *In the special case where β is equal to one and capital demand as well as its net return are fixed, the local government establishes the first-best solution.*

Note that public services are provided efficiently, although the tax rate on capital differs from zero.

If, however, *emissions* are determined by long-term technological investments but capital goods can be adjusted more or less instantaneously, a variation of the tax rates induces the firm to vary its capital demand, while pollutant emissions remain fixed. In this case, τ_k and τ_e are determined so that

$$\frac{\partial \mathcal{U}/\partial P_r}{\partial \mathcal{U}/\partial X} = \frac{\beta - \rho_{\tau_k}\frac{1}{K}\left(\theta\bar{K} - \beta K\right)}{1 + (1 + \rho_{\tau_k})\frac{\tau_k}{\rho + \tau_k}\varepsilon_{p_k}^K} = \frac{\beta - \rho_{\tau_e}\frac{1}{E}\left(\theta\bar{K} - \beta K\right)}{1 + \tau_k\frac{K_{p_e}}{E} + \tau_k\rho_{\tau_e}\frac{K_{p_k}}{E}}. \quad (4.47)$$

Both tax rates are adjusted so that not 'too much' capital is driven out of the region. Contrary to the case where capital is fixed, the tax rate of the inelastically used factor (here: τ_e) does not act non-distortionarily, as one might expect. The reason is that the emission tax has some effect on capital demand and thus on its net return. Under these circumstances, both tax rates are distortionary, and, as is obvious from (4.47), the marginal rate of substitution differs from unity, in general.

It is worth noting that by including environmental aspects, and correspondingly introducing emission taxation in our model, the special case considered in this paragraph is still a generalization of the classical capital taxation model of the tax competition literature.[24] Or to put it another way, if we assume environmental inputs to be fixed, β equal to one, ρ a given constant, and if we do not allow for emission taxation ($\tau_e \equiv 0$), our model reduces to the commonly known model of interjurisdictional tax competition. In this sense, equation (4.38) represents, as a consequence of including pollutant emissions, a generalization of the widely known tax formula:

$$\frac{\partial \mathcal{U}/\partial P_r}{\partial \mathcal{U}/\partial X} = \frac{1}{1 + \tau_k\frac{K_{p_k}}{K}}. \quad (4.48)$$

Obviously, the marginal rate of substitution differs from unity as long as τ_k differs from zero, i.e., as long as the local government has no access to head taxes but has to rely on distortionary taxation. Since in this simple model no other sources of public funds than capital taxation are available to the local government, τ_k is clearly positive. By inspection of (4.48), we see that $\tau_k > 0$ implies that local public goods are underprovided. Recall that in our more general model where regions are identical, one of two different regimes occurs in equilibrium (see page 109). As they are characterized by, among other things, under- and overprovision of public services respectively, the classical tax competition literature exclusively focuses on the first regime, ignoring the second. Recognizing that, in the second regime, overprovision of local public goods may also emerge, the assertion that, in the case of identical regions, local public goods are underprovided need not be true.

If we compare (4.38) and (4.48), we see that in the numerator as well as in the denominator of (4.38) additional terms are subtracted which are both unambiguously negative – provided that τ_k is positive – so that the numerator as well as the denominator increase. Therefore, we are not able to decide whether the marginal rate of substitution between the private and the public good rises or falls, compared to the simpler model without emissions, In other words, if the local government decides to assess emissions by levying a proportional emission tax, it is not quite clear, in general, whether the extent of underprovision of public services is mitigated or exacerbated. Only if τ_k is negative in (4.38), does the introduction of an emission tax yield a clear-cut result: the establishment of a second source of public funds prompts the government to increase the provision of public services *beyond* their efficient level, resulting in overprovision.

4   INTERFERENCE OF THE FEDERAL GOVERNMENT

We have seen that interjurisdictional tax competition leads either to under- or to overprovision of local public goods. The main feature which drives the result is the fiscal externality created by each government. A rise of a local tax rate erodes the tax basis and thereby increases the social marginal cost of public funds. The constancy of the national capital stock implies that capital flight in one region corresponds to an equal increase of the capital stock of the other regions. Therefore, on national grounds, welfare losses in one region and gains in the others have to be weighed against each other. Since local governments ignore exterior benefits, a higher government has to make the lower authorities consider the externalities they create. A common device is either to set fiscal incentives for the local governments to internalize these effects – subsidies or penalties (taxes) – or to try to persuade them to revise their policies in order to achieve a cooperative solution.[25]

4.1   Correcting Interjurisdictional Competition

We show that as long as the federal ministry of finance is not forced to balance public revenue and expenditure, efficiency can be established by an appropriate taxation/subsidy schedule. If local governments levy a positive tax on capital and local public goods are underprovided (Regime 1), the federal government has to subsidize capital taxation but penalize emission taxation. (The contrary is true in the second regime.) To see this, consider, for the purpose of tractability, our model of a small jurisdiction, established in Section 3.2. Suppose that the federal government commits itself to pay subsidies of $S_k(\tau_k)$ and $S_e(\tau_e)$ on capital and emission taxation, respectively. The (local) public budget constraint (4.1) changes to

$$P_i + P_r = \tau_k K + \tau_e E + S_k(\tau_k) + S_e(\tau_e). \qquad (4.49)$$

Because policy variables of higher governments are determined beforehand, the local government, adjusting its policy tools, treats the subsidy schedules $S_k(\tau_k)$ and $S_e(\tau_e)$ as given. Consequently, the first-order conditions of the local government must be modified in so far as within the third bracket terms of (4.22) and (4.23) we have to add $S_k'(\tau_k)$ and $S_e'(\tau_e)$, respectively. By specifying these subsidy terms appropriately, the federal government can ensure overall efficiency.

Proposition 4.8 *Let $\beta = 1$ and ρ be a given constant. If the federal government subsidizes/penalizes capital and emission taxation of the local governments, and the marginal payments satisfy $S_k'(\tau_k) = -\tau_k K_{p_k}$ and $S_e'(\tau_e) = -\tau_k K_{p_e}$, the first-best solution is established.*

Proof: Using $S'_k(\tau_k) = -\tau_k K_{p_k}$, $S'_e(\tau_e) = -\tau_k K_{p_e}$, $\beta = 1$ and that ρ is constant, the first-order conditions for a local government reduce to

$$-U_x K + U_u g' E_{p_k} + U_{P_r} [E_{p_k} \tau_e + K] \;=\; 0, \qquad (4.50)$$

$$-U_x E + U_u g' E_{p_e} + U_{P_r} [E_{p_e} \tau_e + E] \;=\; 0. \qquad (4.51)$$

In this case we get, instead of (4.37) and (4.38),

$$\frac{U_u}{U_x} \;=\; -\tau_e \frac{1}{g'} \qquad (4.52)$$

$$\frac{U_{P_r}}{U_x} \;=\; 1. \qquad (4.53)$$

Equation (4.52) determines the first-best emission tax rate, the Pigouvian tax, resulting in the social optimal emission level. Equation (4.53), on the other hand, ensures optimal provision of local public goods. □

At a first glance, it seems to be curious that, in the first regime, the federal government discourages emission taxation through the imposition of a negative marginal subsidy and, at the same time, encourages capital taxation. But if we recall Propositions 4.4 and 4.6 where we found that, in the first regime, the public revenue is too low but the environmental quality is too high, this result becomes intuitively convincing.

Recall that an increase of τ_e causes pollutant emissions to fall but encourages an import of capital. (See equations (4.20) and (4.21).) Thus, an increase of the local emission tax induces capital flight from the other regions into the domestic region. The federal government seeks to offset this effect by imposing a penalty on emission taxation which is, at the margin, equal to the induced additional tax revenue accruing from an influx of capital.

By introducing the subsidy scheme on capital taxation, the local government is compensated for the marginal erosion of capital triggered by an increase of the local capital tax. Under the subsidy/penalty scheme, each local government acts as if there were no capital flight, and the local regulator no longer hesitates to tax capital more heavily in order to raise public funds. This enables each local government to provide local public services efficiently, although it has no access to head taxation.

If, as is the case under the second regime, the social marginal environmental damage is so high that the revenue collected by the first-best emission taxation exceeds the required first-best revenue, the line of arguments is reversed. Without any interference of the federal government, each local government cuts the emission tax below its first-best level and subsidizes, with the aid of the remaining excess revenue, industrial capital and public goods. Again, this effect is offset by the higher government's policy which discourages capital taxation and subsidizes emission taxation, at the margin.

4.2   Intervention of the Federal Government in the Case of a Symmetric Equilibrium

Another possibile way for the federal government to overcome the inefficiency problem is to initiate a cooperative solution of the local governments. The higher government has to convince the subordinate but autonomous governments to vary their tax rates simultaneously and to achieve a mutual agreement. Unfortunately, a transition from a Nash equilibrium to an allocation that guarantees a higher national welfare level does *not necessarily* imply a Pareto improvement, i.e., a welfare improvement for every region. If, for example, a rise of *all* capital tax rates means that there is a region suffering a welfare loss, we have to expect that, at least, this local government offers political resistance to the proposal of the central government. Let us pursue this case of a symmetric variation of all local capital (or emission) taxes in the ensuing analysis. Clearly, there may be other policy measures which dominate a symmetric variation of either the capital or the emission tax rates. But symmetric solutions seem to be very popular and are often, especially in political bargaining processes, the only enforceable ones. We therefore focus on symmetric solutions here.

Sometimes, regions within one nation are roughly identical with respect to most of their characteristics. In these cases, it seems to be quite reasonable to assume that the preferences of the inhabitants do not differ significantly across the regions (or states) and that the technological standard is almost the same everywhere. This may justify the simplifying assumption of identical jurisdictions. In the subsequent analysis, suppose that the utility functions of the representative consumers and the local production functions are the same in all regions. Correspondingly, the local demand functions are identical and the effects of local tax rates on the national net return to capital are symmetric. But, as often occurs, even within one nation, there are regional distributive differences.

Within the framework of our model, these distributive characteristics are represented by different regional portions of the national capital stock, $\bar{K}$. Hence, we assume that all regions are identical, except that we allow for $\theta^i \neq \theta^j \; \forall i \neq j$. Moreover, so as not to mix up several distributive effects, suppose that the portions of the residents of the local firms are identical, as well. To exclude the possibility of providing public goods at the expense of foreigners, we not only have to assume that $\beta^i = \beta^j \; \forall i, j$, but also that $\beta^j = 1 \; \forall j$. Within this simplified framework we discuss the issue of establishing efficiency by means of an *equal* and *nation-wide* variation of the local tax rates.

Assume that each local government chooses its policy tools under the presumption that it cannot affect national prices, namely, the net return to capital. Taking competitive behaviour of local governments (see also Section 3.2) for granted, we show that, even if all regions are identical – except for their shares of the national capital stock – slight differences of the initial capital endowments may be sufficient to imply opposite welfare effects accruing from a simultaneous increase of all tax rates, evaluated at a symmetric Nash equilibrium.[26] For each region, however, the welfare effect induced by an equal increase of all capital tax rates is opposed to that induced by an equal increase of all emission tax rates. Clearly, as we may expect from the former analysis, the signs of the induced welfare effects depend on the local excess demand of capital and on the question of whether we observe local over- or underprovision of public goods. If, in addition, all regions are identically endowed with capital (in the following 'perfectly identical regions'), the welfare effects of an equal increase of all tax rates are identical for all regions.

In the case of different initial capital endowments, there are losing and winning regions if the local tax rates are increased symmetrically. To see this, we have to differentiate the utility function of the representative resident with respect to all emission and capital tax rates respectively. Denote by $\partial \rho / \partial \bar{\tau}_e$ and $\partial \rho / \partial \bar{\tau}_k$ the marginal change of the net return to capital stemming from an overall increase of the emission tax and the capital tax respectively, evaluated at a symmetric Nash equilibrium. Then, differentiating the capital market-clearing condition yields

$$\frac{\partial \rho}{\partial \bar{\tau}_e} = -\frac{K_{p_e}}{K_{p_k}} \geq 0, \tag{4.54}$$

$$\frac{\partial \rho}{\partial \vec{\tau}_k} = -1. \tag{4.55}$$

Because we know that K_{p_e} and K_{p_k} exhibit opposite signs, the net return to capital does not fall as emission taxes are raised. On the other hand, if capital tax rates are increased by equal amounts, the net return to capital falls by the same amount, implying that capital owners bear the full cost of capital taxation.

Secondly, we need to know how factor demand reacts to an overall tax increase. Therefore, totally differentiate the first-order conditions of some local firm, $R_k = \rho + \tau_k$ and $R_e = \tau_e$, with respect to $\vec{\tau}_k$ and $\vec{\tau}_e$, respectively, and evaluate the result at $dP_i = 0$. By symmetry, an overall and equal change of the tax rates cannot affect the equilibrium allocation of capital, $\partial K / \partial \vec{\tau}_k = 0$ and $\partial K / \partial \vec{\tau}_e = 0$, whereas the change of local pollutant emissions is given by

$$\frac{\partial E}{\partial \vec{\tau}_k} = \frac{1}{R_{ke}} \left(1 + \frac{\partial \rho}{\partial \vec{\tau}_k}\right) = 0, \tag{4.56}$$

$$\frac{\partial E}{\partial \vec{\tau}_e} = \frac{1}{R_{ee}} < 0. \tag{4.57}$$

Equations (4.56) and (4.57) enable us to evaluate the welfare effect induced by a symmetric rise of the emission taxes rates,

$$\frac{\partial U}{\partial \vec{\tau}_e} = -U_x E \left(1 - \frac{U_{P_r}}{U_x}\right) - U_x \frac{\partial \rho}{\partial \vec{\tau}_e} (K - \theta \bar{K}) + U_{P_r} \left(\frac{g' U_u}{U_{P_r}} + \tau_e\right) \frac{\partial E}{\partial \vec{\tau}_e}. \tag{4.58}$$

The first term on the right hand side reflects the inefficient provision of residential public goods. Only if public services are provided efficiently, does this term drop out. In the 'regular' case of underprovision, its sign is positive, whereas in the case of overprovision its sign is negative. The second term corresponds to the region's trade position. If local capital supply exceeds its demand, the sign of the second term is positive; if the region is a net importer of capital, this term is negative. The third term is determined by the level of the local emission tax. Because $\partial E / \partial \vec{\tau}_e$ is negative, the third part is positive if the emission tax is set below its efficiency level, i.e., below the marginal social damage of emissions. However, from (4.42) we know that the emission tax is set too high if, and only if, public services are underprovided. Substituting (4.42) and

(4.57) into (4.58) yields a more concentrated representation of the latter,

$$\frac{\partial \mathcal{U}}{\partial \vec{\tau}_e} = \left[\mathcal{U}_x K \left(1 - \frac{\mathcal{U}_{P_r}}{\mathcal{U}_x} \right) - \mathcal{U}_x \left(K - \theta \bar{K} \right) \right] \left(-\frac{K_{\tau_e}}{K_{p_k}} \right), \qquad (4.59)$$

which immediately gives us the following proposition.

Proposition 4.9 *If in a symmetric Nash equilibrium local public goods are underprovided (overprovided), an equal rise of the emission taxes in all regions implies negative (positive) welfare effects for net-capital-importing (-exporting) regions.*

Proposition 4.9 is somewhat disheartening because, in general, we cannot hope that regions consent to an equal decrease (or increase) of overall emission taxes, although national welfare may be improved. Even in the case of identical regions which only differ with respect to their initial capital endowments, a cooperative solution is not attainable as long as the distribution of capital is sufficiently unequal and side-payments are ruled out. If, however, within each region local capital demand exactly meets local initial capital endowment, we get a stronger result.

Corollary 4.2 *Let all regions be equally endowed with capital, such that within each region local capital supply meets local capital demand. Then all regions gain from an symmetric decrease (increase) of the emission tax rates if, and only if, local public goods are underprovided (overprovided) in equilibrium.*

Corollary 4.2 in conjunction with equation (4.42) says that if in a symmetric Nash equilibrium of perfectly identical regions the provision of local public goods is inefficiently low, the emission tax is set above its efficient level, and the resulting environmental quality is too high (Regime 1), then a Pareto improvement can be attained by reducing the emission taxes in all regions. The contrary is true if public goods are overprovided (Regime 2).

Now consider the welfare effects induced by an equal increase of all local capital tax rates. Similarly, the derivative of the local welfare function with respect to $\vec{\tau}_k$,

$$\frac{\partial \mathcal{U}}{\partial \vec{\tau}_k} = -\mathcal{U}_x K \left(1 - \frac{\mathcal{U}_{P_r}}{\mathcal{U}_x} \right) + \mathcal{U}_x \left(K - \theta \bar{K} \right), \qquad (4.60)$$

exhibits the same terms as in (4.59) but with opposite signs. Hence, compared to the previous case of an equal rise of the emission tax rates, the results of Proposition 4.9 and Corollary 4.2 are reversed.

Proposition 4.10 *If in a symmetric Nash equilibrium local public goods are underprovided (overprovided), an equal rise of the capital taxes in all regions implies positive (negative) welfare effects for net-capital-importing (-exporting) regions.*

Corollary 4.3 *Let all regions be equally endowed with capital such that within each region local capital supply meets local capital demand. Then all regions gain from an symmetric increase (decrease) of capital tax rates if, and only if, local public goods are underprovided (overprovided) in equilibrium.*

Condensing Propositions 4.9 and 4.10 and inspecting equations (4.60) and (4.59), we can conclude the following.

Corollary 4.4 *Each region approves (disapproves) an equal rise of all capital tax rates if, and only if, it disapproves (approves) an equal rise of all emission tax rates.*

Clearly, if all regions are perfectly identical and public goods are initially underprovided (Regime 1), a symmetric increase of all capital tax rates is welfare-improving everywhere; and *vice versa* in Regime 2.

To summarize, we cannot hope to reach an agreement of (almost) identical jurisdictions to overcome the nation-wide inefficiency as long as we focus on symmetric solutions. The reason is that a symmetric variation of either the emission or the capital tax rates does not necessarily imply a welfare improvement in *each* region, if regions differ with respect to their initial capital endowments. Only in the case of perfectly identical regions, can the inefficiency problem be solved by a symmetric cooperative solution.

Under equilibrium Regime 1, where emission taxes are too high but capital taxes are too low and local public goods are underprovided but environmental quality is overprovided, an equal decrease of the emission taxes and an equal increase of the capital taxes induces a Pareto improvement. Similarly, opposite policy measures yield a Pareto improvement under Regime 2.

5 CONCLUDING REMARKS

We have provided a model that integrates, on the one hand, capital taxation as well as the provision of local public goods and, on the other hand, industrial emission regulation within the framework of interjurisdictional competition. The resulting equilibrium tax rates on capital and pollutant emissions lead to inefficient provision of local public goods and environmental quality, in general.

It emerged that the provision of local public goods crucially depends, among other things, on the local initial capital endowment. In particular, the marginal rate of substitution between the private and the public good is strictly increasing in the local capital endowment, whereas the tax rate on capital is strictly decreasing, implying that overprovision is the more likely the lower the (relative) capital endowment. In the special case where local capital demand exactly meets local capital supply, local public goods are underprovided if, and only if, the tax rate on capital is positive.

Environmental quality is 'provided' at inefficient levels as well, in general, and is closely related to the provision of local public goods. Thus, environmental quality is too high if, and only if, local public goods are underprovided. The reason is that the emission tax rate is set above (below) the marginal social damage of pollutants if, and only if, local public goods are under-(over)provided. Contrary to the capital tax rate, the emission tax does not (directly) depend on the local initial capital endowment nor on the region's market power at the national capital market.

For the special case of a small region, we found that only two possible regimes occur. In the first regime, public goods are underprovided, environmental quality is too high, and the tax rate on capital is positive. In the second, public goods are overprovided, environmental quality is too low, and capital is subsidized. Hence, the assertion of the traditional tax competition theory that, in equilibrium, local public goods are underprovided, need not be true. If we allow for emission taxation, this result rather depends on the curvature of the social damage function. For a sufficiently steep damage function overprovision of public goods is accompanied by an inefficiently high level of environmental quality (and *vice versa*).

The higher government, the federal regulator, can establish nation-wide efficiency by applying a subsidy/penalty scheme on local tax rates, if the sufficient public funds are available. For the case of a small region, we found that in the first regime the regulator has to subsidize capital taxation and to discourage emission taxation. The reason is that local governments are afraid of capital flight, so that they refrain from taxing capital more heavily. On the other side, to collect public revenue in order to provide local public goods, they raise the emission taxes beyond marginal social damage. Hence, the central regulator seeks to discourage emission taxation by imposing a negative subsidy. In the second regime, the penalty/subsidy scheme is reversed.

If, however, the federal government has less political power and, there-fore, cannot enforce policy measures which may imply welfare losses in some regions, we can hardly expect efficiency to be established. The rea-son is that, in general, a uniform increase (or decrease) of all tax rates implies opposite welfare effects in different regions. Even though regions are almost identical, i.e., they only differ with respect to their initial capital endowments, local governments prefer different policies. Hence, we get the discouraging result that cooperative symmetric solutions of the inefficiency problem are 'less likely' to be achieved. Only if all re-gions are perfectly identical, can Pareto improvements be obtained by cooperative symmetric behaviour.

NOTES

1. Recently, a few papers have dealt with this topic. For example, Oates and Schwab (1988), van der Ploeg and Bovenberg (1993a,b), Bovenberg and van der Ploeg (1993), and Schneider and Wellisch (1994) integrate fiscal and environmental policy within an interregional setting. In these works, however, the aspects of fiscal federalism and of interjurisdictional competition play only a minor role. In particular, possibilities for a fed-eral government to re-establish efficiency by correcting the equilibrium outcome remain disregarded and unexplored.

2. To illuminate the effects of induced capital movement, we do not consider real externalities, i. e., pollution is assumed to be purely local.

3. Some of the models mentioned above are included in our specification as special cases. In particular, we derive a generalization of the tax formulae

given by Zodrow and Mieszkowski (1986), cf. eqs (20) and (29).

4. This need not be true if the federal ministry of finance has to equate exactly public revenue and expenditure, and lump sum transfers are not available.

5. In their classical paper Zodrow and Mieszkowski (1986), analysed tax competition where local governments provide either residential or industrial public goods. Since both public goods induce quite different welfare effects, and, from an empirical point of view, each of them exhausts a significant portion of total public spending, we incorporate the simultaneous provision of two public services.

6. Note that this simplification is not essential for our results. If we model the provision of public goods by specific production processes instead of specifying them as public purchases of private goods, the results remain qualitatively unaffected.

7. The portion $1 - \beta$ of the profit of the local firm belongs either to residents of other regions or to foreigners.

8. We can think of an exporting firm whose local sales are so low compared to its world-wide sales that they can be ignored. For the case where local firms produce the single consumer good, see, for example, Kennedy (1994). (See also the previous chapter.)

9. The analysis could easily be adapted to the case of a small competitive firm which has no impact either on factor or on output prices. The important point is that the local firm fully anticipates the equilibrium price effect that is induced by a change of its output. If, however, the behaviour of other competitors induces second-order price effects that have to be taken into account by the local government, the analysis becomes more untractable; but the main results remain true for any market structure.

10. Here and in the remainder of this chapter the dot stands for the omitted, fixed arguments. (In this case, for p_k, p_e, and P_i.)

11. Keeping this in mind, we no longer refer to K, E, Q, and p as *equilibrium* values, though we always consider these variables along the equilibrium path of the output market. This convention enables us to attach the word 'equilibrium' to the outcome of interjurisdictional competition and the related variables, unambiguously.

12. Apparently, (4.9) is a somewhat uncomfortable 'joint condition' on F. But note that by concavity F_{ke} is restricted in absolute values by $|F_{ke}| < \sqrt{F_{kk}F_{ee}}$, anyhow. Therefore, (4.9) is only binding if the inverse demand curve is 'almost too convex' in the sense that

$$0 \geq 2p' + p''Q > -\frac{\sqrt{F_{kk}F_{ee}}}{F_k F_e}(p + p'Q),$$

otherwise (4.9) is non-binding.

13. Alternatively, in the case where ρ is exogenously given, we can write factor demand as functions of the tax rates: $K(\tau_k, \tau_e, \cdot)$ and $E(\tau_k, \tau_e, \cdot)$.

14. As in the previous chapters, we are not able to prove the existence and uniqueness of an equilibrium of interjurisdictional competition, in general.

15. If, however, we allow for pollutant transmission, this is no longer true due to real externalities.

16. The positiveness of this term within the brackets means that the cross-price effects of the factor demands do not outweigh its own-price effects, or, roughly speaking, that each price change induces the strongest demand effect on its own item.

17. More precisely, the denominator of (4.28) is smaller than $1 - (1 + \rho_{\tau_k})(E_{p_k}/E_{p_e})(E/K)$ if, and only if,

$$\tau_k > -E_{p_k}\rho_{\tau_e}K\frac{det(Hess(R))}{1 + \rho_{\tau_k}} \quad (< 0).$$

18. In deriving (4.31) and (4.32) we have used the fact that

$$K_{p_e}\rho_{\tau_k} - K_{p_k}\rho_{\tau_e} = K_{p_e}\rho_{\tau_k}\left(1 - \frac{K_{p_k}}{K_{p_e}}\frac{K_{p_e}}{K_{p_k}}\right) = 0.$$

19. An analogous result for τ_e can be derived by setting $d\tau_k$ equal to zero.

20. Instead of dealing with a small region, we may alternatively examine the case of identical regions (including identical initial endowments). In this case, capital demand must meet capital supply in each region. However, the assumption of a small region is slightly stronger than that of identical regions.

21. A similar result can be derived when there is also an output effect. If local residents consume the output of the local firm, positive direct welfare effects accrue from local production. (Refer to Chapter 3.)

22. In the special case where environmental quality is just the negative of aggregated emissions – g' is equal to minus one – we have $\tau_e = U_u/U_x$, which is a widely known familiar result of optimal emission taxation.

23. Capital consumers (firms) bear the full cost of increasing the tax rates and thus of extending the supply of local public services. If, on the cont ry, we have $\partial\rho/\partial\tau_k = -1$ and $\partial\rho/\partial\tau_e = -1$, capital owners bear the full burden of (additional) taxation.

24. See, for example, Zodrow and Mieszkowski (1986), Wildasin (1988), ar 1 Hoyt (1991b).

25. Clearly, if the federal government is authorized by law to determine the local tax rates directly, neither a subsidy scheme nor persuasion is required. In federal states, however, for a couple of tax rates – especially

for capital and emission tax rates – the legislature is given to subordinate jurisdictions.

26. Although other equilibria may exist, we focus on a symmetric equilibrium. In this case, the initial capital endowments do not have any effect on optimal tax rates, given by (4.41) and (4.42). Because factor demand is the same in all jurisdictions, each local government imposes the same tax rates and thus provides the same quantity of public services in equilibrium.

5. Conclusion

Throughout this work we have investigated interjurisdictional competition and its equilibrium outcome. Particular interest was focused on the provision of public services and on the prevailing environmental quality. To deal with this topic, three different models exhibiting increasing complexity were calibrated. Our starting point was the simple model introduced by Zodrow and Mieszkowski (1986) and Wildasin (1988). In Chapter 2 we modified their approach by considering public goods that benefit industry, not residents. While in the classical tax competition literature public expenditure is financed through capital taxation, we focus on emission taxes in Chapter 3. Both approaches are integrated into a single model encompassing capital and emission taxation as well as residential and industrial public goods in Chapter 4.

These models allow us to analyse interjurisdictional competition in more detail. Its equilibrium outcome depends crucially on the specification of the strategic variables and on the characteristics of public services. It makes an immense difference whether, firstly, governments engage in *tax* or in *expenditure* competition or whether, secondly, governments provide *residential* or *industrial* public goods. Moreover, there is a strong interdependence between the resulting equilibrium environmental quality and the provision levels of public services. Since, within a second-best framework, each tax rate serves, among other things, directly to finance public expenditure, the provision of public goods hinges on the steepness of the social damage curve, reflecting consumers' propensity to pay for a better environmental quality. Therefore, a deliberate specification of the available policy instruments and of the intended use of public revenue is indispensable.

Since a major part of the interjurisdictional competition models is crudely specified, results are rigorous and indiscriminate. For example, the traditional literature suggests that interjurisdictional competition leads, on the one hand, to underprovision of public goods and, on the other hand, to a too low environmental standard. Moreover, it is commonly believed that interjurisdictional competition in public expenditures is 'more competitive' than in tax rates – if this strategic difference is recognized at all. However, our first simple model (Chapter 2) makes two of these results break down. We show that, even if we neglect the environmental problems, the traditional results may be reversed if we consider industrial public services: in some polar cases interjurisdictional competition in tax rates is 'more competitive' than competition in public expenditures, and public goods are underprovided under the tax regime but may be *over*provided under the expenditure regime.

The approach presented in Chapter 3 considers taxation of industrial pollutant emissions which serves to finance public goods, exclusively. Again, it turns out that the widely spread result that emission taxes fall short of local marginal environmental damage is not necessarily true. If, in equilibrium, public funds are sufficiently scarce, the emission tax exceeds local marginal environmental damage. Similarly, it may even occur that a local government fixes its emission tax above nation-wide marginal damage.

The model of Chapter 4, the most general one, encompasses two tax rates, the provision of two local public goods, and the prevailing environmental quality. The results of our previous models remain true within this fairly general model. Public services and the environmental quality are provided at inefficient levels, and both are closely related through the tax system. In the special case of a small region, we have the striking new result that only two possible regimes occur: we have either under-provision of public goods and a too high environmental quality or the opposite is true. Hence, the assertion of the traditional tax competition theory that in equilibrium local public goods and environmental quality are underprovided need not be true, and is even false in some special cases. However, in most regular cases, we have to expect that local public goods are underprovided and that the environmental quality is too low from a nation-wide viewpoint, at least if pollution is transboundary. Nevertheless, the important finding is that the opposite may also occur. In any case, interjurisdictional tax competition leads to an inefficient provision of local public goods and environmental quality, in general. The equilibrium allocation is neither Pareto- nor second-best efficient. The reason for the latter is that, due to fiscal and real externalities, local governments face incentives to deviate from cooperative behaviour. Thus, to establish the constrained optimal allocation requires the intervention of a higher (federal or multinational) government. To achieve this, several policy measures have been presented.

To sum up, although the concrete equilibrium outcome of interjuris-dictional competition hinges crucially on a deliberate calibration of the model, this work supports weakly the hypothesis that interjurisdictional competition leads to underprovision of public services and to 'ecological dumping'.

References

Aschauer, David Alan (1989), 'Is Public Expenditure Productive?', *Journal of Monetary Economics*, **23**, 177–200.

Baltagi, Badi H. and Nat Pinnoi (1995), 'Public Capital Stock and State Productivity Growth: Further Evidence from an Error Components Model', *Empirical Economics*, **20**, 351–359.

Barnett, A. H. (1980), 'The Pigouvian Tax Rule under Monopoly', *American Economic Review*, **70**, 1037–1041.

Barrett, Scott (1994), 'Strategic Environmental Policy and International Trade', *Journal of Public Economics*, **54**, 325–338.

Baumol, William J. and Wallace E. Oates (1988), *The Theory of Environmental Policy*, 2nd ed., Cambridge: Cambridge University Press.

Bayındır-Upmann, Thorsten (1995), 'Interjurisdictional Tax Competition, Provision of Two Local Public Goods, and Environmental Quality', *Finanzarchiv*, **52** (NF), 379–400.

— (1998a), 'Two Games of Interjurisdictional Competition when Local Governments Provide Industrial Public Goods', *International Tax and Public Finance*, **5**, (forthcoming).

— (1998b), 'Interjurisdictional Competition in Emission Taxes under Imperfect Competition of Local Firms', *European Journal of Political Economy*, **14**, (forthcoming).

Beck, John H. (1983), 'Tax Competition, Uniform Assessment, and the Benefit Principle', *Journal of Urban Economics*, **13**, 127–146.

Bovenberg, A. Lans and Ruud A. de Mooij (1994a), 'Environmental Levies and Distortionary Taxation', *The American Economic Review*, **94**, 1085–1089.

— (1994b), 'Environmental Taxes and Labor-Market Distortions', *European Journal of Political Economy*, **10**, 655–683.

Bovenberg, A. Lans and Frederick van der Ploeg (1993), 'Green Policies and Public Finance in a Small Open Economy', Discussion Paper No. 9335, CentER for Economic Research, Tilburg University.

— (1994), 'Environmental Policy, Public Finance and the Labor-Market in a Second-best World', *Journal of Public Economics*, **55**, 349–390.

Brander, James A. and Barbara J. Spencer (1985), 'Export Subsidies and International Market Share Rivalry', *Journal of International Economics*, **18**, 83–100.

Bucovetsky, Sam (1991), 'Asymmetric Tax Competition', *Journal of Urban Economics*, **30**, 167–181.

Bucovetsky, Sam and John D. Wilson (1991), 'Tax Competition with Two Tax Instruments', *Regional Science and Urban Economics*, **21**, 333–350.

Burbidge, John B. and Gordon M. Myers (1994), 'Population Mobility and Capital Tax Competition', *Regional Science and Urban Economics*, **24**, 441–459.

Conrad, Klaus (1993), 'Taxes and Subsidies for Pollution-Intensive Industries as Trade Policy', *Journal of Environmental Economics and Management*, **25**, 121–135.

Conrad, Klaus and Jianmin Wang (1993), 'The Effect of Emission Taxes and Abatement Subsidies on Market Structure', *International Journal of Industrial Organization*, **11**, 499–518.

Davies, Stephen W. and Anthony J. McGuinness (1982), 'Dumping at Less than Marginal Cost', *Journal of International Economics*, **12**, 169–182.

Dixit, Avinash (1984), 'International Trade Policy for Oligopolistic Industries', *Economic Journal (Supplement)*, **94**, 1–16.

Eaton, Jonathan and Gene M. Grossman (1986), 'Optimal Trade and Industrial Policy under Oligopoly', *Quarterly Journal of Economics*, **101**, 383–406.

Ebert, Udo (1992), 'Pigouvian Tax and Market Structure: The Case of Oligopoly and Different Abatement Technologies', *Finanzarchiv*, **49**, 154–166.

Endres, Alfred (1983), 'Do Effluent Charges (Always) Reduce Environmental Damage?', *Oxford Economic Papers*, **35**, 254–261.

Ethier, Wilfred J. (1982), 'Dumping', *Journal of Political Economy*, **90**, 487–506.

Frank, Charles R. and Richard E. Quandt (1963), 'On the Existence of Cournot Equilibrium', *International Economic Review*, **4**, 92–96.

Friedman, James W. (1977), *Oligopoly and the Theory of Games*, Advanced Textbooks in Economics, Vol. 8, Amsterdam: North-Holland.

Gordon, Roger H. (1986), 'Taxation of Investment and Savings in a World Economy', *American Economic Review*, **76**, 1086–1102.

Goulder, Lawrence H. (1995), 'Environmental Taxation and the "Double Dividend": a Reader's Guide', *International Tax and Public Finance*, **2**, 155–182.

Gramlich, Edward M. (1994), 'Infrastructure Investment: A Review Essay', *Journal of Economic Literature*, **32**, 1176–1196.

Hoyt, William H. (1991a), 'Competitive Jurisdictions, Congestion, and the Henry George Theorem', *Regional Science and Urban Economics*, **21**, 351–370.

— (1991b), 'Property Taxation, Nash Equilibrium, and Market Power', *Journal of Urban Economics*, **30**, 123–131.

International Monetary Fund (1994), *Government Finance Statistics Yearbook*, Volume XVIII, Washington, DC: IMF.

Jensen, Richard and Eugenia F. Toma (1991), 'Debt in a Model of Tax Competition', *Regional Science and Urban Economics*, **21**, 371–392.

Johansson, Olof (1994), 'Optimal Indirect Taxation in a Second-best Perspective with Regard to Externalities, a Public Budget Restriction and Distribution Effects', mimeo, University of Göteborg.

Kennedy, Peter W. (1994), 'Equilibrium Pollution Taxes in Open Economies with Imperfect Competition', *Journal of Environmental Economics and Management*, **27**, 49–63.

Krutilla, Kerry (1991), 'Environmental Regulation in an Open Economy', *Journal of Environmental Economics and Management*, **20**, 127–142.

Levin, Dan (1985), 'Taxation within Cournot Oligopoly', *Journal of Public Economics*, **27**, 281–290.

Markusen, James R. (1975), 'International Externalities and Optimal Tax Structures', *Journal of International Economics*, **5**, 15–29.

Markusen, James R., Edward R. Morey, and Nancy D. Olewiler (1993), 'Environmental Policy when Market Structure and Plant Locations are Endogenous', *Journal of Environmental Economics and Management*, **24**, 69–86.

— (1995), 'Competition in Regional Environmental Policies when Plant Locations Are Endogenous', *Journal of Public Economics*, **56**, 55–77.

Mintz, Jack and Henry Tulkens (1986), 'Commodity Tax Competition

Between Member States of a Federation: Equilibrium and Efficiency', *Journal of Public Economics*, **29**, 133–172.

Mooij, Ruud A. de and A. Lans Bovenberg (1995), 'Environmental Taxes, International Capital Mobility and Inefficient Tax Systems: Tax Burden vs. Tax Shifting', mimeo, OCFEB, Erasmus University Rotterdam and CentER for Economic Research, Tilburg University.

Musgrave, Richard A. and Peggy B. Musgrave (1989), *Public Finance in Theory and Practice*, 5th ed., New York: McGraw-Hill.

— (1990), *Die öffentlichen Finanzen in Theorie und Praxis*, 5th ed., Tübingen: J. C. B. Mohr (Paul Siebeck).

Oates, Wallace E. and Robert M. Schwab (1988), 'Economic Competition Among Jurisdictions: Efficiency Enhancing or Distortion Inducing?', *Journal of Public Economics*, **35**, 333–354.

Pethig, Rüdiger (1994), 'National Emission Tax Policies, Competitive International Trade in Final Goods and Allocative Repercussions', mimeo, University of Siegen.

Ploeg, Frederick van der and A. Lans Bovenberg (1993a), 'Environmental Policy, Public Goods and the Marginal Cost of Public Funds', *The Economic Journal*, **104**, 444–454.

— (1993b), 'Direct Crowding Out, Optimal Taxation and Pollution Abatement', Discussion Paper No. 9365, CentER for Economic Research, Tilburg University.

Rauscher, Michael (1994), 'On Ecological Dumping', *Oxford Economic Papers*, **46**, 822–840.

— (1995), 'Environmental Regulation and the Location of Polluting Industries', *International Tax and Public Finance*, **2**, 229–244.

Requate, Till (1993a), 'Permits or Taxes? How to Regulate Cournot Duopoly with Polluting Firms', in: L. Preisner (ed.), *Institutions and Environmental Protection – Conference Proceedings of the 3rd Annual Meeteing of the EAERE*, Vol. 2, Krakau.

— (1993b), 'Pollution Control in a Cournot Duopoly via Taxes or Permits', *Journal of Economics*, **58**, 255–291.

— (1994), 'Green Taxes in Oligopoly Revisited: Exogenous versus Endogenous Number of Firms', Working Paper No. 234, Institute of Mathematical Economics, University of Bielefeld.

Richter, Wolfram F. and Dietmar Wellisch (1993), 'Allokative Theorie des interregionalen Finanzausgleichs bei unvollständiger Landrentenabsorption', *Finanzarchiv*, **50**, 433–457.

Sandmo, Agnar (1975), 'Optimal Taxation in the Presence of Externalities', *Swedish Journal of Economics*, **77**, 86–98.

Schneider, Kerstin and Dietmar Wellisch (1994), 'Capital Mobility, Trade, and Optimal Environmental Policy', mimeo, Dortmund University.

Statistisches Bundesamt (1995), *Statistisches Jahrbuch 1995 für die Bundesrepublik Deutschland*, Stuttgart: Metzler-Poeschel.

Takayama, Akira, (1985), *Mathematical Economics*, 2nd ed., Cambridge: Cambridge University Press.

Tiebout, Charles M. (1956), 'A Pure Theory of Local Expenditures', *Journal of Political Economy*, **64**, 416–424.

Ulph, Alistair (1992), 'The Choice of Environmental Instruments and Strategic International Trade', in: R. Pethig (ed.), *Conflicts and Cooperation in Managing Environmental Resources (Microeconomic Studies)*, Berlin: Springer, Ch. 5, 111–132.

— (1996), 'Environmental Policy and International Trade when Governments and Producers Act Strategically', *Journal of Environmental Economics and Management*, **30**, 265–281.

Viner, Jacob (1931), 'Cost Curves and Supply Curves', *Zeitschrift für Nationalökonomie*, **111**, 23–46.

Wellisch, Dietmar (1995), 'Locational Choices of Firms and Decentralized Environmental Policy with Various Instruments', *Journal of Urban Economics*, **37**, 290–310.

Wildasin, David E. (1988), 'Nash Equilibria in Models of Fiscal Competition', *Journal of Public Economics*, **35**, 229–240.

— (1989), 'Interjurisdictional Capital Mobility: Fiscal Externality and a Corrective Subsidy', *Journal of Urban Economics*, **25**, 193–212.

Wilson, John D. (1985), 'Optimal Property Taxation in the Presence of Interregional Capital Mobility', *Journal of Urban Economics*, **17**, 73–89.

— (1986), 'A Theory of Interregional Tax Competition', *Journal of Urban Economics*, **19**, 296–315.

— (1987), 'Trade, Capital Mobility, and Tax Competition', *Journal of Political Economy*, **95**, 835–856.

— (1991), 'Tax Competition with Interregional Differences in Factor Endowments', *Regional Science and Urban Economics*, **21**, 423–451.

Zodrow, George R. and Peter Mieszkowski (1986), 'Pigou, Tiebout, Property Taxation, and the Underprovision of Local Public Goods', *Journal of Urban Economics*, **19**, 356–370.

Index